MURDERING POVERTY

How to fix aid

Arrey Elvis Ntui

First published 20 February 2016
Published by Sanaga Press
ISBN-13: 978-1530 – 19 - 698 - 2 (paperback)
ISBN-10: 153 – 0196 - 981

Contact: arreyelvis(@)gmail.com
www.twitter.com/arreymcntui

Murdering Poverty – How to fix aid

Dedication

To Veronica Ndip Ntui (RIP)
Who will forget a mother's love?

Contents

Preface

Why this kind of book?

I wanted this book really short. Development professionals, researchers and students have several hundred policy documents to read. This book should not add to that burden. There is an emergency here. Rather than spending several days worming your way through papers on development, I felt you'll be better served with a book that goes straight to the point with ideas you could start considering for changing the way development aid works right from your next day at work.

Donors and beneficiaries (visible and hidden) should not dismiss development aid critics with a wave of the hand. We should listen to understand the issues and address the concerns in order not to perpetuate the failure. Murdering Poverty – I hope – is the aim of development aid. It is the object of this small book.

The several million people in the world who generously donate to charity have a right to understand why progress has stalled, despite their benevolence. More importantly perhaps, they should find in this book a reason to hope. Hope that their hard-earned money can be channeled in smarter ways to achieve outcomes charities claim they are out to produce. Global giving has hit 150 billion dollars per year since 2014. But the pale dividends have understandably lead to aid's critics running a scream campaign against most foreign aid.

Where does this book fit? This book is about development, development economics and international relations if you wish. But to me, this is first and foremost a book on creativity. I won't be quoting tonnes of research by social scientists to buttress points here. This is not that kind of book. As such, this book is deliberately written simple (– I hope). Simple people with a good heart and good intentions are putting their treasures to lift others out of poverty. They deserve to be told a simple story. Let us try to avoid another tyranny of experts. These people who support charities with their donations, their country's development agency and multilateral agencies through the taxes they pay should not be milked routinely for the same meager results.

Development is for everybody, not just for think tanks, development specialists, PhDs, charity people and international relations experts. This work shows some application of creativity to solve political, economic, social and international relations problems related to development. It is about opening the reader's eyes to see that there are non-academic ways of addressing the current development challenge of lifting people out of poverty for good. By applying a little bit of creativity, we can change the face of development aid for ever.

In this small book, I suggest several initiatives for turning around development aid. Some of them are radical, others are plain commonsense. But I am aware commonsense doesn't always work in politics. There are some bold suggestions here. One or two of them may throw you into a fit and have you stamp this book against a wall, wrestle its pages or smack your screen. But aid professionals and policy makers will have to be bold. A few economic ideas influencing the dispatch of foreign aid will be jostled or trampled upon. Such has been the depth and breadth of failure that Angus Deaton's analysis reduces aid to a 'holding operation'. (Deaton, 2010). What a fitting recognition for underperformance! It is time for new thinking.

How about agreeing that development aid is some form of payment for hidden or undefined services which developing countries might be providing the world? How about trimming the fat off mammoth agencies like the UN and other self-deifying charities in favour of issuing development aid directly to individual beneficiaries? Could a wholesale rejection of aid on moral principles by recipient countries provoke donors to enter a soul searching mission on themselves to question their motives, results and effects? Would the reciprocation of aid balance the global aid industry and guarantee sustainability in a way that taxpayers around the world get reasonable value? Should donor countries be focusing aid money on themselves, to address the fundamental structural failings in their own countries that perpetuate the need for global development aid? Should donors be guilty for taking the bulk of financial benefits from development aid so far? What changes in aid governance and models does Africa need?

Is there an ideal foreign aid model? Could *Chufle,* the Churchill-Fleming aid model be the long sought gold standard?

Coping with poverty's three chamber guillotine

The poor do not always make bad choices. They are victims of poverty's three chamber guillotine. Death by attitude. Death by lack of money. Then death by institutional failure. I will explain.

Poverty runs a two chamber system of sniffing life out of people or perhaps even three. In the first chamber, it is their attitude to problems as poor people. In the second, it is the absence of the means, even when they had the right attitude. In the last chamber, it is the environment.

Poverty is a very sophisticated system of thought, action and beliefs.

Poverty creates a belief system of its own. It doesn't usually matter much if the poor are Christian, Muslim, follower of some African traditional creed or Jewish. The openly acknowledged religion of the poor is distorted decision making and analysis produced by poverty induced adaptations.

The poor and the rich will read one bible passage. Get them interpret it to themselves. The rich will use the passage to enhance their condition, support their lifestyle, authenticate their individual views and invalidate what others might think of them, their material dispositions and future hopes in their faith. The poor will do exactly the same thing: comfort themselves in their condition, reinforce their belief there is no point worrying for everything will be okay and that their lack of assets and its resultant labours is fine and perhaps enviable for their religious promise to mature.

Kill People Prematurely: How Does Poverty Do It?

Late in the year 2015, I watched a scene in a Nollywood movie that portrayed something terrible about poverty, health scares and near tragedies that adorn the lives and souls warped in poverty.

A Nigerian teenager had just been rushed to a half decent medical facility by her mother and his senior sister. The small private clinic as among the makeshift institutions that form the shaky backbone of the health system in several rural locations in Igbo land.

The boy has an emergency. This panic-struck family has managed to transport him this far: at the front office of the clinic. The two nurses behind the reception desk are unimpressed by the two women's shrill voices pleading for an urgent intervention.

"Please, call the Doctor! Where is the doctor?"

"Madam, stop making noise here! You are disturbing our patients", responds the professional in white garment.

"Call the doctor my brother is dying", she weeps as a high fever throws the boy into a fit.

The nurse who had been chitty-chatting with a colleague lazily opens a big book and readies her pen. "Where is your consultation fee and deposit?"

"Please, help oh, help oh, doctor!" The boy's mother adds. "So there is no help here for poor people?"

"Madam, this is not a government hospital. You have to pay first!" The nurse said coldly.

She let her brother's body half on the floor and half in her mother's hands. With trembling fingers she counted notes from a bundle she'd just pulled out from the cleft under her bra.

Eventually after the payment, a doctor came, the boy was hospitalized, drugs administered and his life saved. But before the doctor left, the relieved mother took one final shot at him.

"So doctor, does it mean that if we are poor, we cannot get treatment?"

The doctor smiled. "Madam, your son will be alright. We've administered him drugs. Life is money. We have costs to cover, staff to keep and bills to pay. Your son is well now. We thank God."

*   *   *   *   *

This brief movie scene on Africa Magic's epic channel offers a glimpse into poverty's inner workings. Living in poverty in any of the several dozen developing countries where social safety nets are zilch shuts you out of medical care. But it works in at least two stages.

When people live in poverty in many African countries, they adopt certain attitudes which are meant to help them adapt to their financial reality. But paradoxically, these same survival tactics can be their ultimate undoing. The poor teach themselves to ignore symptoms of disease. That's stage one of poverty's two chamber execution. In this chamber a headache, a fever, an ailment is underlooked by default. This is mental poverty. A state of poverty that flourishes as an attitude induced by lack of resources. A poor family would reason that seeking medical advice could end up costing them like 10 dollars for precautionary malaria and fever drugs.

It is not exactly that they cannot find 10 dollars to spend on health at this stage. Rather, those living in poverty tend to think they can shrug off the fever and that any money spent would have been wasted on speculative medication.

By the time they finally understand it is serious enough to warrant medical help, it is usually too late.

In poverty's second execution chamber, the poor adopt the right attitude to a health alert. The poor would decide to go to hospital irrespective of how much money the whole health visit might cost. They might just have 10 dollars but belief it is a more profitable investment in their chance of survival than saving it for say the next day's food. By this choice, the poor escape poverty's first death chamber. And perhaps that will just be enough to get them going until they finally escape poverty or manage to sneak their way through life cheating death every now and then.

Poor people make bad choices, but not all the time. Poverty operates a two or three chamber destroyer system. Chamber one: the poor are reluctant to seek a doctor (attitude). In chamber two, the poor decides to see a doctor, speculatively. In doing so, they escape early death in chamber one. In this second chamber however, the medical expert prescribes medication. The poor do not have the money to buy or faced with other priorities like food, medication is on the basis that money is left over. In a country where there are no reliable social safety nets, the poor would ultimately succumb to their illness and take their grave early.

In the optional third chamber, the poor manages to find a Samaritan relative who can cover some medical costs. The drugs are unavailable or the medical expertise is lacking. The poor still die. Principally because they cannot afford an evacuation to a medically advanced country. This third chamber is institutional poverty. The poor cannot escape it, except for the extraordinary intervention of the First Lady, the President of the Republic or some philanthropist of billionaire-like proportion. How can the poor escape all three chambers?

Chapter I Development Aid at Crossroads

An apple in the tree that mocks a fallen fruit must have missed the lesson on gravity.

Eliminating poverty with foreign aid is one policy area everyone seems to be failing at. The Millennium Development Goals phased out in 2015. The world has agreed Sustainable Development Goals for another period of trials that follow. Clearly, development aid is not scheduled to end soon. Dreamy statements from statesmen about the possibility of ending poverty within a generation by applying development aid are just what they are: dreams.

Aid will mutate. Some countries will need a decreasing amount of aid after a certain climax. But unless several states suddenly made discoveries of huge diamond, gold or gas deposits underground and run the affairs of the nation with wisdom, probity and selfless benefit for present and future generations, development aid still has long life, life measurable in centuries, not decades. And even for those who make an Ali Baba find, we'll have to hope those precious minerals and gases are not bewitched enough to take the country backwards into wars of brotherly attrition.

The Development Challenge

Hundreds of millions of people have escaped extreme poverty over the last three decades. Another 1.4 billion people remain. That's not a good statistic. That is not the only problem. Experts these days are segregating poverty into two or three or more branches. Extreme poverty, poverty and perhaps the poverty of the working poor, with the last one being totally orphaned at worst. At best they are subject matter for left wing politicians to quote enough to wiggle their way up to power in an election.

The potential for misallocating progress in beating down extreme poverty (reducing the number of people living on less than $1.25 a day) to development aid efforts is high. It is tempting and the Bono clan may use it to foster the creed. Development aid's contribution to alleviating poverty has been slim, sporadic or its extent questionable. China ignored the MDGs but still lifted 680 million people out of poverty between 1980 and 2010. Growth was the key. Not aid. Growth will remain the key to lifting people out of poverty. But aid remains useful. It just should take a new aim. It should simulate the behavior of economic growth. Development aid should help support the infrastructure for enabling growth. Aid should reach beneficiaries. Aid should create wealth.

Even as an insignificant fraction of developing countries escape the massive need for aid in the future, it is not unthinkable that some European countries which erstwhile had bracketed themselves rightly or wrongly among developed countries will need more and more 'development aid' as their economies slide in a fiercely competitive world. Events in Portugal and Greece between about 2010 to 2015 are clear pointers that development aid could mutate (or has already done so) in a new direction. That may be some way off. But it is not inconceivable. Aid will live. Politicians and policy makers will quarrel over what new name to give to it, over how to administer it, but aid will exist in some form. Even giants might someday need aid. Looking back, the Marshall Plan isn't that far off.

Will the rich, when *Birnam wood*[1] starts to move, and they fall from grace, accept that new crown bearers administer global development aid to them they way it is done currently to developing countries? It is perhaps of an absolute necessity to maintain the debate on the mechanics of aid in order to find the situation specific solutions that beat text book prescriptions.

And talking of textbook specifications, those on development aid maybe deserve a brutal trial. Such has been the failure and questioning of aid that there is great room for sensationalist expert development economists to make small fame from good or bad noise on the topic. As a student of economics, you shrug in despair when you first hear that normative economics is the stuff where all experts are right, could be all right or all wrong and could be all wrong. Those who faint at the sight of varsity proclaimed economics experts who never ever get one prediction right can take some consolation. The subject of development aid is not far off.

---

[1] Birnam wood – In 'Macbeth', a play by William Shakespeare, following a prophecy, Birnam wood started to move to mark the shift in power from the reigning monarch to a rebel group.

Of aid evangelists and aid demons

Aid has been questioned, challenged and even condemned in some cases by critics and campaigners, among them Thembisa Moyo on the one hand; hailed, implored and even 'rightified' by donors and activists, among them Bono and Geldof on the other hand.

As the last few candles of the MDGs burned out, development aid entered a storm of scrutiny- with the well shared view that it has failed in too many respects and too many places, especially in Africa. Development aid is in the emergency unit of the world's progress hospital. Some of the best minds in business and government have been drawn to the operating table, out of compassion or necessity: Bill Gates, Tony Blair and a growing host of political management and industrial talent. By December 2015, the Bill and Melinda Gates Foundation had spent 34.5 billion USD on global development. The aid money balloon keeps growing. But as its growth fails to justify, its foes take aim.

Dambisa Moyo argues *"…aid is a silent killer of growth…"*. This is a strong statement, a blowing remark, an intense conclusion but a thesis worthy of further and continuous scrutiny. You could see aid as food. You eat to live (I hope), like most people I know. Food is normally a good thing. You starve, you die. Period. But food kills, despite being primarily meant for sustaining life. Eat contaminated food and you're off to the doctor's. Eat too much, in combination with other life factors and you'll die of blocked arteries, heart disease, cholesterol choking or a near cousin. So, food kills. But this would not lead us to condemn food as slow poison or would it? But if Moyo means that aid is a silent killer of growth in the same way food is everyone's silent killer, she's certainly correct. But still, food is a silent healer for so many people.

Like food, development aid is neutral. It only becomes negative or positive depending on additional factors, the nature, timing and purpose of aid a country consumes. It's just like food. In principle, aid is good, not bad and certainly not wholly a silent killer of growth. It's more like a badly administered pill. Bad doctor. Bad pharmacist. And a patient who so blindly trusts in medical experts that he fails to challenge the prescription. Aid recipient countries have failed to challenge the development aid mechanism. Or their governments are simply in complicity with the rich doctors.

Criticism of development aid has been varied and sustained, finding favourable echoes in certain western newspaper columns.

"The notion that aid can alleviate systemic poverty, and has done so, is a myth. Millions in Africa are poorer today because of aid; misery and poverty have not ended but increased. Aid has been, and continues to be, an unmitigated political, economic, and humanitarian disaster for most parts of the developing world," Dambisa Moyo. *8 Jan 2011, The Telegraph, www.telegraph.co.uk*

"This is the vicious cycle of aid. The cycle that chokes off desperately needed investment, instills a culture of dependency, and facilitates rampant and systematic corruption, all with delirious consequences for growth …. However foreign aid perpetuates poverty and weakens civil society by increasing the burden of government and reducing civil freedoms …. Foreign aid does not strengthen the social capital, it weakens it …. In the world of aid, there is no need or incentive to trust your neighbour, and no need for your neighbour to trust you …. Which is why foreign aid foments conflict. The prospect of seizing power and gaining access to unlimited aid wealth is irresistible.'
Moyo, Dambisa

Several newspaper columnists have commented with enthusiasm on 'study after study' which have found aid to be ineffective, unreliable and producing results not worthy of efforts invested. There is significant conviction that big flows of foreign money promote corruption, breed conflict and make nonsense of democracy by encouraging poorer countries to place more emphasis on donor demands than on the legitimate desires of their people. South Africa's panic protest reaction when Britain announced it was ending aid to the country in 2014 may be worth investigating as the typical kind of government reaction that supports the pessimist premise of aid. Pretoria's anger at the United Kingdom announcing an end to a circa £20 million per year aid programme feels like a grenade in the hands of those who suspect irresponsible governments have an unholy lust for 'free money' from taxpayers in foreign countries. But that is perhaps a matter for another day.

It has been reported that Angus Deaton, a former aid evangelist has turned against the 'aid illusion'. Deaton is an economics professor at Princeton and a renowned poverty economist. He frowns at government aid policies that just sustain an aid industry that allows those who burn aid money have moral superiority over the rest. (Deaton, 2013) Development aid is akin these days to a new religion, ripe with its crowd of zealots, mild faithful, backsliders, bigots, heretics and rebels hungry for a reformation in an industry that is itself unrepentant despite claiming to work to bring positive change to others.

It won't be wise to dismiss development aid's critics though. On very close examination, several of development aid's most fervent critics are people who have taken notice that aid might have become a huge beast of an industry that serves other purposes- mainly undisclosed or at least not publicly acknowledged - rather than sustainable development. Not the development of struggling countries as we would ideally have. The rise to the limelight of development aid's detractors is directly proportional to the scale of failure of most aid and the disillusionment that has befallen some of its erstwhile fervent enthusiasts.

Aid has become such a beast that it would be attempted career suicide for mainstream politicians to venture to halt it. Understandably. Alongside few but undeniable successes like in controlling the spread of HIV/AIDS, the rise of the aid critic is arguably one of development aid's biggest achievements over the last decade. But even in this, it appears aid is failing. There are too few vocal critics of aid. Voices so weak that the industry is successfully shrugging off any attempts at reforming it. Instead, it is getting bigger at the same time that there is the realization that too many benefits are accruing to the donor, instead of the recipient. Giving aid is sexy as an idea. Who has time to bother whether aid is achieving sufficient 'sexy' returns?

Should We Fear The Third Sector?

Development aid is like a chameleon that changes its colour to blend in the environment in which you find it. In developing countries in Africa and Asia, it appears at face value to be delivering much needed support to ailing systems and a better life for the people. Western media have already convinced us that things are bleak on the African continent and in several backward Asian countries. Despite some coming to terms – albeit slowly- that African countries are havens of opportunity, the old ragged, wretched view of the continent hangs on.

Basic life support systems and social safety nets are appalling. Blood gurgling dictators have confiscated vast natural wealth for themselves, their cronies and a small clique of failed western educated technocrats who help keep the status quo. Hollywood and Broadway stars have donned UNICEF ambassadorial tunics and are crusading to bring peace, educate girls or feed the starving multitudes on African soil. Retired businessmen, whose net worth surpasses the GDP of whole countries, are resolved to doing 'God's work' and Africa is their theatre.

Wasted politicians, usually from rich donor countries themselves, have found a new calling, a new mission to be evangelists for development. There's news of a civil war in the offing there, a looming famine here, rigged elections in the backyard and potential for a coup within sight. So any aid announcement is a sign of hope that learned benevolent foreigners are coming with help.

Aid is there to bring positive change and plug the numerous gaping holes in the development infrastructure of failing, near failed, struggling or failed states. At least you should believe so. If not, why else is it being continued? The premise is that aid is helping the right things happen. That's a good thing, though it remains questionable how much benefit accrue overall. When you look at the animal called development aid in donor countries like the United States, the United Kingdom, France, Germany, Australia and Canada, you cannot help but see a massive industry employing millions of people.

Employment too is a good thing, isn't it? The charity/aid sector is called the 'third sector' in the public life in rich countries. The first sector is the public sector or government. The second is the private sector or business. Now there is a third sector. A massive one. But one which has yet to reach its peak. It ensures jobs for millions and sprinkles cold water drops of hope on the poor's forehead. So aid benefits both the rich donor countries and should benefit the poor recipient ones in Africa and Asia. So in whose interests will it be to end aid?

Development aid is at a crossroads – maybe even at a vicious roundabout. In this respect, oil might even fare better. For oil, there is broad agreement that there are better options for generating clean energy: solar, green and other renewables. Its remaining challenge is to make the options become more economically attractive than oil and much faster too in addition to nailing some commonsense into the heads of stubborn politicians and profiteering capitalists. That is beginning to happen. The climate agreement at COP21 in Paris presented an additional legal incentive to steer away from reckless use of fossil fuels.

For development aid, consensual better options are scant, if not absent at all. Apart from calling for more and more aid dollars to be poured into the global development aid machinery and wondering whether aid for trade could be the magic drug, there isn't much in the way of reforming development aid. It is left to everyone's imagination to fathom what will happen when aid is finally doubled by countries which want to meet the 0.7% target of GNI spend on overseas development assistance.

The ease with which poverty is dismissing the efforts of some of the best people and their financial resources probably warrants a more radical surgery of the aid mechanism. In this book, I explore some new premises, programmes and channels to rewire aid for more effectiveness. I challenge some of the theories on which aid has been founded up till now. The ideas that follow will address accessibility, transparency, sustainability, equity and effectiveness of development aid. You would expect that with all the aid that has gone into Africa over the years now, significant progress should have been made. That has not been the case. Why does development aid fail?

Chapter II The 24 sins of development aid

The unexamined life is not worth living. – Socrates according to Plato

It might be useful to freshen up on some of the shortcomings which have led to the tough questioning around development aid. But before delving into these, let's be clear that despite the negative publicity that aid generates in some – or in fact in a growing number of quarters these days, not all aid has failed. Development aid has played a massive positive role in managing the HIV/AIDS pandemic. It is regrettable that there hasn't been more success nor have development professionals really found a way of translating the relative success in handling the spread of HIV into a formula for success in other development initiatives. Development aid has its numerous issues.

1 Its purpose is not clear, mistaken for CSR

Most of what is pushed around today as development aid qualifies flat for Corporate Social Responsibility which governments of countries and their charities toss around the world to appease the losers and earn a false halo on their crown. Unfortunately, that is the way several politicians see it in their minds. In many instances, donors and recipients will struggle to see aid other than as CSR and that immediately creates problems for the effectiveness of aid.

2 Most development aid is not whole-hearted

You can see when aid is insincere. It is true that some aid is so full of décor you won't immediately see its intended or unintended hypocrisy. Aid that picks and chooses problems to tackle, with little or no understanding of the real issues, aid that is really nothing but a dollar amount, aid that is inflexible and that doesn't put the human experience as a core concern of its delivery – that's half-hearted aid. And such aid doesn't work. Its benefits – if any – will be eroded in a very short time. And usually, that is what happens with much of development aid.

When you examine some aid programmes, you cannot help but ask, 'do they really want to solve these problems?' Donors would know on several occasions that an aid intervention is just there so that it appears the wealthy country is doing something. In other cases you can sense a psychological unease in the funding government's approach. A fear lingers that if they definitely solve this or that problem, the beneficiary could become a competitor for higher goals. And so despite the sexy large sums of money being fire-worked as aid packages, an intricate fear of the unknown mechanism tends to inhibit the process and extent of interventions which could solve poverty for good.

Do not expect donors to agree with this. But this hidden fear complex appears to be at the route of almost all donor induced malfunctions and sources of inefficiency in the aid mechanism to address poverty.

3 Massive corruption

Old constant but probably the easiest to resolve. The quality of governance in aid management can only be equal to the governance quality of the government and civil society structures that manage development aid. Civil society will more often than not respond to requests for transparency or feel compelled to a high standard of responsiveness and execution which governments can just laugh off as it disappears in their massive bureaucratic mechanisms.

To compound matters, the principle of sovereignty and non interference has crept into it, making it less likely for donor countries to sufficiently challenge recipient governments as to the use of aid. It is even more difficult to challenge aid use when it is being disbursed by a multi-lateral agency, over which contributing countries themselves have lost all control to international civil servants and the interwoven moral hazard of international consultants and contractors.

As consultants usually have well anchored links to donor countries, it becomes even less attractive for questioning unless there are significant failures or disagreements.

4 Aid goes back to the donor

Some researchers find that as much as 30% of development aid finds its way back to donor countries. Others have campaigned against aid with the argument that donors put 100% into Africa and squeeze out 140% making developed countries reap the net benefits of development aid instead. These arguments are not unfounded. Investments to End Poverty reports that in 2011, rich countries 'donated' 150 billion dollars in aid. Of this, only 59 billion dollars were traceable as having actually been cash transfers to recipient governments, NGOs operating on the ground and other field programmes in beneficiary countries.

Target dates to untie aid have been missed. Large amounts of aid money never leave rich countries. Development aid figures can be deceptive. Homi Kharas (2007) states in a working paper that not all aid money can be applied to development projects. In fact, to get the actual amount of development aid reaching beneficiaries, the Country Programmable Aid or CPA, you have to subtract the administrative costs of aid agencies, emergency and humanitarian relief and technical assistance from the aid figure. Technical cooperation is more like staff salaries of rich donor country citizens working as development advisors and consultants.

Humanitarian relief and emergency aid are understandable, especially if the disasters did not result from initial development failings or even if they did. That aside, it is clear that the cost of running big multilateral, bilateral and massive charities is taking up money that could otherwise be allocated to actually building schools, training teachers, nurses and teaching business skills to beneficiaries. Kharas contends that where all country programmable aid to poor country governments amount to 38 billion dollars, only circa 19 billion dollars actually gets to final beneficiaries.

How does aid money find its way back to donors? Huge salaries for expatriate aid workers in Africa through international multilateral organisations and international NGOs, via corruption when unscrupulous officials embezzle development funds to stuff them in foreign bank accounts or pay for expensive holidays in America and Europe.

Big development banks – including the World Bank – systematically opt for international competitive bidding, notes the report, increasing the chances that large firms from donor countries will eventually win the contracts. Half the contract value of World Bank-funded projects in the last decade went to companies from donor countries. In 2008, 67% of World Bank-financed contract amounts went to firms from just 10 countries. It is very easy to guess which those 10 countries are.

In an interview granted to the United Kingdom's Guardian newspaper in 2011, Claire Provost cites Uganda as an example where only 18% of the financial value of World Bank funded projects was obtained by firms operating locally. As the contract value rose to one million dollars, the local business share percentage dived to 11%. Chinese and British firms won the majority of deals from World Bank-funded programmes in Uganda in that year. China got 32% and the UK 19%. In effect, development aid was being used to prop up the economies of China and the

United Kingdom. Poor Uganda! They where only a window dressing!

A paper in the Journal of Economic Perspectives written by Easterly and Pfutze (spring, 2008) highlights administration costs of some aid donating organizations as a percentage of their ODF (Official Development Financing) as follows: Asian Development Bank, 8%; African Development Bank, 12%; UNICEF, 14%; European Bank for Reconstruction and Development, 15%; Caribbean Development Bank, 26%; IFAD (UN), 22%; IMF 75% and Global Environment Facility, 75%. It doesn't stop there. The paper suggests that several international organisations employed in the fight against poverty spend a disproportionate amount of money to administer themselves than they give as development aid to the poor.

Multilateral aid at 12% and all aid at 9% still shows that too much money destined for aid is 'lost' in the administrative structures of donor organizations. The two researchers conclude their paper warning that the data they had access to might be flawed, were murky and regretted that such affairs concerning help to the poorest was not being given the consideration it deserves.

Another research trumpeted by the Guardian newspaper in 2014, raised controversy as it was found that only a minor fraction of aid to agriculture given by the Bill & Melinda Gates Foundation had found its way to Africa. The bulk of that foundation's aid to agriculture went to US and European organisations. It might be necessary to point out that the Bill & Melinda Gates Foundation is a private organization and is not bound by OECD rules when giving out aid. However, that distribution apparently echoed similar self-service bias as it happens with aid issued by national governments of developed countries.

You would think it is obvious that Africa and its millions of famine struck inhabitants would be the primary beneficiary of any agriculture-related pots of money. Not always the case. But as a private spender of privately generated aid funds, it should be of little concern where and on whom such money is spent. This simply underlines some of the conditioning with which even well meaning private donors have entered the global development market.

Development aid recipient countries are not the priority for aid cash transfers.

5 Changes the burden of responsibility

Critics of development have pointed out that Africans should be allowed to bear responsibility for their own development and their own failings which resulted in their underdevelopment. They argue further that aid breeds corruption and irresponsibility. Whether Africans and their goings and coming are solely responsible for their plight is a subject beyond the scope of this book.

However, we learn that aid does something terrible. It shifts the expectation and responsibility for progress which people should normally place on their local leaders from these locally elected or appointed officials to rich countries. In some instances, the mental dependence on developed countries for aid can be so high within a population that people fold their arms, don't blame their lame leadership but instead clamour to the 'international community' for solutions to their problems.

The expectation of foreign aid perpetuates irresponsibility and absolves those who run local affairs with bad governance. It gets people to stop thinking. Instead of making connections and tweaking tools and processes to find improved solutions to local issues, local leaders and their communities surrender and wait to surrender further to a foreign imposed solution to their challenges.

It can get worse. In several instances, the local population mistake development aid from some foreign government or private oversea benefactor as evidence of progress obtained by some lackluster country president. Aid enables bad leadership to earn the sympathy and political credits of local people which should be rather directed to the original benefactors. In doing so, aid allows local politicians to fiddle with local taxpayers money that should be directed to funding socio-economic projects for the development of the community in the hope that aid has made up for it.

The streets of some African countries – mostly dictatorships veiled as growing democracies – are adorned with banners exalting and glorifying presidents after the inaugural opening of hospitals and schools built by Korea, Japan and China. The same goes for the only properly tarred roads funded by the European Union. Aid funded projects genuinely help several people use a proper hospital or tarred road for the first time. But its by-product is praise for regimes which have confiscated their country's tax basket and natural resources for themselves and a clique of civil servants who pretend to emulate Western development ideals. The common citizen is left to hang their hope on the largesse of Europe, the US, Canada, Korea, Japan, China, Australia and others.

'Mr Ambassador, we need farm to market roads. Our children cannot go to school because a storm stole away the roofs of the only three usable classrooms we had. The filtering system of our community-funded water supply has been clogged by dirt for three months now. Your Excellency, we count on your ... ."

You would pity these ambassadors who tour their host countries. The things they hear surely make them wonder if people thought they are contesting for the next election in that country. Such has been the misdirection of political requests for development.

Development aid contributes to one of the foremost governance scandals ordinary citizens of underdeveloped countries could be spared from. What is the morality in river water over-blessed Kenya, Nigeria, Cameroon and several dozen others accepting development aid to run or fix their countries' water supply systems nearly half a century after their independence? So what have these budding 'democracies' been doing with tax money paid by their citizens?

Is it sensible that any foreigner should be paying for simple water to be served to anyone in 'stable' Cameroon, a country where over 80% of the administrative divisions are named after large rivers sweeping through the country with leisurely arrogance and beauty?

How come any country in the spoilt-for-water Congo Basin and Great Lake regions of Africa looks out to foreign aid to make clean water flow in taps? Aid fosters the dictatorship of a pointless democracy where failure is rewarded instead of being sanctioned.

6 Incomplete

Most times, development aid is so partial, so narrowly focused that other failings in the system of the aid recipient community simply drown out any benefits or progress made in that sector by aid money. It's a case of problems growing faster than solutions can cope with. While the ills of underdevelopment grow geometrically, the benefits from development efforts sometimes only progress arithmetically such that the gap to plug keeps widening, despite everyone's 'best' efforts.

It's like someone suffering from malaria, typhoid, a broken limb and a sore throat. The development aid operation is like a clinic that threats nothing other than broken limbs. Plus the way in which donors run programmes means that even the broken limb may not be treated until it fully heals.

Then, even if they manage to stay until the limb is cured, aid is hardly there to eliminate the root factor that caused the broken limb. Maybe it was a badly built staircase, a ride on a bike as the passenger of an unlicensed rider, getting hit crossing the road at a junction with no zebra crossing or traffic lights which no one respects. This is not to suggest that aid should be blamed for not developing countries. It is more of recognition that the current ideology surrounding aid is centred on the premise that development aid should not solve a problem to any reasonable depth.

7 Has no soul: nothing but a figure

A good deal of development aid is being administered these days as financial targets. Rather than targeting both qualitative and quantitative objectives which can and should demonstrate that progress has been made, aid picks what it is willing to spend, irrespective of what it would really achieve. When you fix development aid contribution to say 0.7 percent of a country's GNI, which is even hardly ever met by anyone, you just run the risk of potentially destroying the essence of governance and the democratic systems in place for citizens to hold leaders in aid recipient countries to account. Once rogue dictators know that a pack of misguided wealthy countries have set aside money to clear the mess in their countries, what would encourage them to clear the mess by their own means?

According to the OECD, only a handful of countries were on target in 2013 to meet or exceed the target of 0.7% of GNI spend on Official Development Assistance. This included Norway, Sweden, Luxemburg, Denmark and the United Kingdom. (OECD, April 2014). Development aid has been converted to a tax ceiling.

The current aid target model prioritizes the amount spent over the results achieved. In this approach, it is not what a donor country achieves in developing others that counts. What is important to the OECD aid donor cartel is how much they spend. There is no correlation between amount spent and development objectives attained. This reading of the target 0.7% and the interim targets which lagging donors have fixed for themselves or managed to achieve, could result in donors digging and refilling trenches and earning marks thereof for spending development money.

8 Complicated

You hear of large sums of money lying in trust funds or central banks destined for development and at the same time hear in conferences how this and that country has been unable to access and deploy those resources for development. For several years, Cameroon was not able to access money sleeping in the Congo Basin Forest Fund financed by the UK and Norway and unable to access billions of francs the French government had purportedly stocked in trust funds for development aid destined to Cameroon.

These are scandals of complication. And in the meantime, donors move around from one conference to the other, blaming governments for not putting forth adequate bids to access development money which is lying in wait for them. If a development fund is so complicated that beneficiaries are unable to access more than 50% of it in a given time slot, chances are that the funder is playing other games or has so badly planned its development aid programme that it is simply fit for the trash can. By hamstringing aid access with several bureaucratic hurdles, donors destroy the trust that anyone has on the sincerity of purpose of aid. The onus is on the funder to find the necessary channels to deploy committed development aid. Otherwise it was senseless to even pledge and stockpile the money in the first place.

9 Aid has created a perverse incentive

It has created a massive industry that has to ensure that aid fails for it to survive. Aid orchestrates its own failure. Development aid creates several million white collar jobs for Europe, America and the other donor countries. Someone has joked that to end development aid now would mean to make millions of Europeans and Americans jobless. There is a reason why this is so. Aid is a game that benefits the donor six times more than it benefits the beneficiary. The aid industry is among the biggest sectors in the economies of the UK, Germany and the USA.

It is the revered third sector. It plays God every now and then, torturing the spirits of others, heaping guilt and demanding more charity money. Poverty fighting charities have fashioned themselves as the moralizing material arm of society, where the public sector is at the mercy of re-election-mongering governments and the private sector at the ever growing mercy of profiteering shareholders.

10 Silly attempt to replace fair trade with aid

Development aid attempts to skip the real issue. The more important issue to address is injustice in world trade. Europe and America are illegitimately protecting many parts of their industry like agriculture in a manner that ensures Africa cannot compete and then turning around to offer food aid, to put it bluntly, atone for international political sins. Rich countries pride themselves in how many million dollar worth of aid they have 'generously' contributed to development efforts. If we changed the way aid contributions are calculated, to take into account subsidies to home economies, reverse flows and all other actions which help create the need for aid in the first place, we could end up with a more realistic figure like 'net aid contributions'. We will certainly have much fewer or no countries at all meeting or nearly reaching their development aid targets.

11 Outdated education for development 'experts'

A look at some of the elite Anglo-Saxon universities which train many of the professionals at postgraduate level who manage or contribute to existing policy on development aid reveals a course content which is rich in economic theory and socio-political content. A typical course in development or any of its variants is comprised of a combination of the following core courses: aid and development, economics, econometrics, environmental economics, sustainable development, international (financial) institutions, project planning, African development, political economy of development, public policy and administration, politics, conflict, peace and security. While these courses in themselves are rich and can form the basis of a rigorous academic training, they are essentially a mistake if they are meant to train the people to help Africa combat poverty.

The general academic training offered by these courses and their relatives is undisputable. But they are a long way off from preparing professionals to deal with the dynamic problems facing the developing countries in Africa, for example. The development challenges in failing third world countries will not be resolved by cramming half century old economic theories and dated clichés about Africa. Even if theories are dusted in new books and offered in new formats and supported by academics under the client-spell of the very international institutions whose policies are the most trumpeted, they do nothing but add to the spiral of failure in which many developing countries are trapped.

Those willing to dedicate their careers to resolving development issues should rather get a thorough grounding in creativity and innovation. Developing nations need solutions – some of which have not been tried before elsewhere – sometimes totally new ways of making change and progress happen. There is little or no evidence that the solution to the developing world's problems are written in any existing textbook or hidden in any of those university courses.

The processes which have worked in the West do not have an automatic ticket to success in failing countries, especially those of Paul Collier's Bottom Billion. Embarking in development and poverty alleviation has to be seen more and more as an entrepreneurial mission and postgraduate courses rooted in entrepreneurship and the open spirit of innovation may be better suited preparatory training for the daunting and exciting adventure of developing countries where decades and countless programmes of the IMF, World Bank, UNDP and several hundred charities and NGOs have failed to make lasting sustainable impact.

A master of science in innovation, creativity and entrepreneurship content appears a stronger preparation for the new Africa than the content of development studies at famous and popular universities. At the very least, schools like the School of Oriental and African Studies, University of Birmingham, Yale and the rest should put forth a new development programme at master level comprising a hybrid of their current development studies offering and the excellent problem solving courses in the innovation, creativity and entrepreneurship masters at Newcastle University, City University London and Buffalo State for example.

12 The budget cycle, short-termism and the craze to throw money

Donor governments, their funding agencies and embassies telling recipients 'we can only fund a three-month training programme, we don't have time' when everyone knows that that programme needs a minimum of nine months to deliver any effective benefits. Donors are chained to a slave god with a double-edged sword. While the diktat of the national budgetary cycle ensures that officials are obliged to spend funds allocated to aid, it also opens the doors for pre-meditated failure to be embedded in projects and programmes.

13 The administrative burden of aid sucks up aid

Give some money to an organization and ask them to go to a community in a developing country and run something as simple as a scholarship scheme for a given target group of beneficiaries for example. Many organisations could take anything from nine to 18 months to draft the terms of reference, recruit personnel and conjure sets upon sets of paperwork. That could take anything from 10 to 50% of the intended aid money.

Where the aid amount is so small that the admin costs could suck up to 90% of it, organisations would turn it down or just gulp it in admin in the hope that a second funder will provide the actual aid money. You can understand why huge organisations suck up funding in the admin drain. Concern to be seen not to mismanage public funds is sometimes the overriding objective in these organisations. The effectiveness and efficiency of development programmes can sometimes fall lower in the priority order. Where compliance requirements overrides development objectives, money is spent just doing that: complying.

14 Politicians not understanding aid

You may have wondered whether politicians both at the giving and receiving ends really know the contours and inner workings of aid. Development aid is a political orphan. Leaders don't know it until they arrive power, except for very few exceptions. Aid is not a sexy topic for elections like immigration, economy, war and social benefits. The impact of politicians' not understanding aid? The aid portfolio is left in the hands of sect-like aid activists within the government machinery.

Prior to elections, it is fairly standard what line most politicians have in their head about aid. Give aid if we have the money, if we can be seen to try to meet commitments set by my stupid predecessors or where public opinion is overwhelmingly in favour of aid. Or just give aid to keep hungry would-be migrants away from our shores and polish up our image in the assembly of civilized nations.

Politicians on the giving side have groomed themselves to accept that being overly critical of aid whilst not being politically incorrect can be socially incorrect. Those who even bother to criticize aid only do so if they can propose alternatives that sound like something else but actually mean aid with a different name or stranger mechanisms for its implementation. Recipient politicians on the other hand have their palms itching for development aid money as a default.

It would be interesting to see what happens if government of a developing country that comes up with a policy that does not permit the state, except in declared emergencies, to accept budgetary aid. Development aid is not something on which election manifestos dwell. As a consequence, the effectiveness of development aid is really no country leader's Holy Grail. Not that you can blame them for this. Responsibility for development lies first and foremost in the hands of Africans and citizens of other developing countries.

15 Trojan horse aid

Development aid recipient governments fearing civil society will outplay them using aid has led them to place hurdles that impede the effectiveness of aid and leads to a waste of resources. Many governments believe certain aid projects are attempts to bypass their authority, subvert them and operate a rival government, an illegitimate administration, self appointed and anointed by faceless foreign agitators.

In most of these countries, dictatorial systems have muted the opposition and any dissenting voices. They see aid flowing through civil society as western attempts to plant the seeds of a revolution or create a more effective opposition.

Many democracy and human rights projects are victims of Trojan horse suspicions.

16 Key stakeholders marginalized in the aid chain

Many developing country governments do not necessarily at all times represent the best interest of their people. This has been known for a long time. But aid money keeps pouring into the hands or pockets of thieving governments. They already have tax money to steal. Tax money is even actually money belonging to citizens. If governments can steal tax payers' money with no qualms, you should be surprised at how peacefully their consciences and superficial systems of checks and balances lie as they grind money that clueless foreigners have classified as development aid.

Local people who are supposed to be beneficiaries are treated like toddlers who can only cry when hungry but cannot say clearly if a snack or milk is what they want. The local councils watch central government administration – often based in the capital city totally cut off from provincial realities – negotiate and receive aid money which hardly flows downstream. Civil society who should be vocal observers and watchdogs of propriety for the poor's sake are treated with fear and suspicion like traitors in waiting.

17 Badly negotiated aid: donor imposed priorities

This is how aid priorities are decided: a few high thinking politicians from 'big schools' tell some experts from some think thanks or donor country ministerial department about their lofty goals for failing Africa. They discuss how they could use aid money to transpose their 'values' to Africa. The experts knock down these ideas into objectives around which those who are interested in helping the developing world take a step in the right direction must now warp projects.

You'd hope it makes sense. Development experts from the best research universities in the West brainstorming and deciding what works best for hundreds of millions of people on a continent that eludes anyone's control and full understanding. He who pays the piper calls the tune. Unfortunately, the overwhelming evidence is that it doesn't work like that in development. Developing peoples don't have all the answers but they best know what is good for them. Setting priorities from the donor's point of view rather than the beneficiary's most likely leads to missed opportunities.

Usually though, the donor's think thank has some bright ideas. Developing countries are faced with several problems in various socio-economic and cultural contexts. Experts can think great but perhaps beneficiaries are those properly qualified to rank priorities and solutions in order of magnitude and preference. Aid money comes with a significant moral baggage and that's a problem for recipient communities. The moral baggage influences what solutions donor experts are comfortable with. The local community often has its own moral influences. These influence the choice and ranking of priorities, usually in favour of what western trained experts find less sensible. Those universities, courses and textbooks again.

18 Broken coordination

Several actors in a cacophony – Giving aid is now a competitive business. It's like another form of capitalism, except that there are hardly any market regulators. All you have is business saints all claiming to their creator that they are relevant. However, there is a certain amount of joint funding. That is usually when the saints realize their individual halo is not big enough to cover the sins of the beneficiary or when they find the wisdom to share the risks of failure. Several aid programmes are so structured that when not run by a multilateral organization, disparate financial calendars and regulatory constraints can constitute 'natural' and insurmountable barriers to cooperation and coordination.

19 Biased dismissal of hardware aid

There is only a very small number of western donor organizations that offer even a limited amount of hardware aid. Several more explicitly forbid beneficiaries from buying hardware with their aid money. These 'software-only' funds argue that beneficiaries will usually steal or divert hardware like vehicles and computers for personal use. It is funny how they see it. And beneficiaries are finding it difficult to catch up with the reasoning. What's easier to steal: cash or hardware? The results are significant. They include an insipid display of seminars and conferences funded by aid dollars that yield little fruit. The final consequence is even worse: a postponement of the real solution to the problem the aid package actually set out to address in the first place. And this just perpetuates the aid dependency cycle like an addiction.

Software bias is in the ranks of poor prioritization. Wrong prioritization of aid money has led to suspicious reading of the development aid agenda. How can you explain that for all the hundreds of millions of Euros the European Union has spent in Cameroon for example, there is not a single hospital built with EU money while one decent hospital can go for under 10 million Euros? Is it not surprising or telling that for all the recognition of the pivotal role education should play in development, not one western donor bothers to build a decent high school, small university college or vocational institute in an average African country? It could be argued that it is not the role of western governments to build schools and hospitals for developing countries, while they themselves struggle to meet their own home needs. If this is true, so what then is the purpose for spending billions of dollars in development aid?

20 Trying to do too many things with money

Aid money is sometimes like an overworked mule. Donors brandish a tiny sum of money and then instead of focusing it to achieving one or two sensible outcomes, they expect development planners to work magic in gender, women's health, human rights, primary health care, security, economic empowerment, education and access to water. Aid dilution leads to programmes achieving progress that gets washed away because the tap root never sunk deep enough. Donors and recipients are often deceived by the lively colours of having a wide range of feeble impact projects. Allocating the finite resource of development aid packages to fiercely competing priorities continues to be a challenging undertaking for development professionals.

21 Development aid at the service of donor home economies

Africans often wonder whether Switzerland and European Union countries would ever like to see and support an African industry of fine finished African chocolates of exquisite quality. It is a competitive world and maybe it is not Bern's or Brussels' problem if others have not understood the trick. You should not be surprised why it is much easier for an African group of farmers or rural common initiative group to get support from rich donor countries to improve their cocoa farms, enhance the quality of the beans and hygienic conditions under which they are exported than they can get for setting up a small chocolate processing plant.

Development aid appears to have as one of its aims the maintenance of a certain economic status quo. Producers of cheap raw materials on the one side. Tertiary producers and manufacturers of value added and overpriced finished products on the other side. In an extreme sense you could say development aid, its direction of flow and biased thematic areas effectively constitutes a bribe to stay lazy and get Africans keep off the more lucrative side of business. One of the great tragedies of development aid is that of employing itself to sustaining the continuous economic subjugation of recipients to donors.

22 Selling after the market

There is an unfortunate tendency in administering development aid that consists of trying to address issues in 'recipient' or 'beneficiary' countries long after they have turned worse. Aid tends to come when repairs needed are most costly, more disruptive, late or almost. Development aid waits sometimes for years of statistics to be amassed before it budges. By the time aid comes, problems have usually morphed into something else. As such, aid addresses problems that no longer exist in the form in which 'experts' understand. Most aid is currently scheduled to be reactive rather than proactive. Aid almost waits for signs of a genocide before sending in the 'experts' to help disgruntled peoples manage their economic resources and political affairs in an equitable and peaceful way.

23 Inflated objectives

There has been widespread failure to recognize that development aid has more or less been nothing but a holding operation. By design or accident, aid has served to help stop situations getting worse. Some efforts have been sincere but expectations have been mismanaged. When designing projects and programmes, everyone tends to exaggerate the objectives and the outcomes. This temptation is so strong because if people don't do this, fund managers will not be exited enough to give the necessary green light to release the money.

The consequence is that when programmes are long concluded, the promised benefits are hardly anywhere to be seen. So the enemy press of development aid steps in to trump the mess and clamour for a death sentence to aid. Aid does not deliver massive improvement, at least going with the level of resources currently in place. Due to efficiency losses in an aid programme's circuit and environment, it principally stops things from getting worse and secures earlier benefits. But keeping the status quo sounds like a lame marketing pitch for the active forces in the aid industry. So the industry promises more and delivers an anti-climax, despite it actually delivering some minor benefits.

24 Quite plainly, aid fails

There is little or no correlation between aid and socio-economic indicators. Liberia unfortunately is a sad illustration of this. Here is a country that has received huge amounts of money as aid for more than a decade. According to the Organisation for Economic

Cooperation and Development, official development aid to Liberia exceeded three quarters of a billion dollars in 2011, amounting to 73% of the country's GNI. In other years, Liberia got even larger amounts from the aid drip. The year 2013 illustrated how much aid failed to improve educational outcomes in the country. In that year, 25,000 students took the entrance exam into the University of Liberia. Everyone of them failed in what has become known as the epic fail.

All the aid the country received was not able to provide half decent education to a single Liberian secondary school leaver. In another gory human development statistic, Liberia is among the bottom pack of countries with the worst doctor to patient ratio. In 2015, roughly 20% of the country's 261 registered medical doctors were foreigners. That gave it 1 doctor to 19,000 patients, much better than what it was after doctors fled the Ebola outbreak in 2014. To put things in perspective, Zimbabwe at the same period was estimated to have 1 doctor for 8,000 patients and Nigeria 1 to 4,000 patients. Worse, Liberia, a country of less than four million souls had only two pediatricians for its one million children. It feels like the aid money has been well spent.

It is of no import whether education was a target area for aid spending. On whatever priorities you spend nearly one billion dollars in a small country, you will expect ripple effects to touch education. That aside, if education was not earmarked for aid spending, who made the decision on what Liberia's priority areas should be? Ten percent of Liberia's aid package could produce and employ 140 doctors annually but it didn't. The result: Ebola.

Development aid as it stands has its problems. Over the past four decades, policy makers have been working on solutions to clear the underdevelopment that has continued to characterize several countries of the world despite significant progress by rich ones. One of the articles of faith widely touted as a panacea to lift countries out of poverty is the call for advanced countries to contribute 0.7% of their Gross National Income (GNI) to development aid. It is worth examining the basis and worth of this facility in the fight against poverty.

Chapter III Will 0.7% GNI Contribution to Aid End Poverty?

There are only two types of money problems: too little money and too much money.

Laudable efforts are being made by a few countries to commit a sizable chunk of their GDP to helping developing countries, the 0.7% target. Britain has become one of only five countries (as at 2015) hitting the hallowed target. The others are Norway, Sweden, Luxembourg and Denmark. It is baffling to imagine the size of fund flows in the global aid industry when others like the United States, Germany, France, Japan, Canada and Australia finally commit to and actually meet that target.

You would think 0.7% is a new god to whom all morality soaked development advocates and some of the world's leaders are paying allegiance and religious devotion to. You can be forgiven for that.

The Origin of 0.7% GNI target

Is 0.7% of GDP sufficient for development aid?

It is worthy to delve briefly into the history of the 0.7% GNI aid target. What is the origin of 0.7% objective the world is so glamourously chasing? Could its wide acceptance be a product of the gone-past-sell-by-date development programme courses at SOAS, Yale, Birmingham, New York and others? Or is it just a case of acceptance for lack of something better?

The idea that rich countries should donate 1% of their national income to help develop the world's poorer nations was first put forth by the World Council of Churches in 1958. (Christian Concerns in Economic and Social Development, August 21-29, 1958, Appendix XIV, p. 125. – cited in OECD, Development Co-operation, 1999 Report). So clearly, the idea was to replicate the religious tax of tithes reminiscent of what happens in synagogues and certain Christian churches.

This 1% target included both private and public aid flows. It was calculated that private aid flows could account for 0.3%. Private flows would be then future money dripping down the likes of Hellen Keller, Bill Gates Foundation, Mo Ibrahim Foundation and thousands of others appalled by public failures and feeling a heart-wrenching need to stake their wealth and that of others as bailout for those in dire need. As such, the Pearson Commission proposed the public aid target at the United Nations General Assembly in October 1970 at 0.7%.

It is important to note that agreement on the target was by no means easy. It took several meetings, debates and tight cross-examination for the target to be formally recognized by a UNGA resolution in 1970. Agreement to be bound by the prescriptions of the target has been queried, rejected, twisted, squeezed or mauled by many countries at one time or the other. But according to the OECD, "it has been repeatedly re-endorsed at international conferences on aid and development down to the present day." However, the combined contribution by donor countries to aid has hardly ever exceeded 0.4% of their combined GNI. But failure to reach the target is maybe not the point.

The setting of 0.7% GDP as target spend for development aid is both intriguing and worrying. It has drawn praise from several quarters. In a 2015 interview granted to Euractiv.com, Norbert Neusser, a German politician from the Social Democratic Party regrets that his country is failing to meet the 0.7% development target. Neusser even takes it further, drawing analogy from the rich countries' failure to reach the development aid target as evidence that climate targets agreed (in Paris in December 2015) will just as well not be met.

The aid target has become some sort of Holy Grail of development programming for rich nations who pride themselves in and are apt to brandish it at international conferences as game trophy for their global social responsibility and generosity to the world's sick, lagging and failing states.

The problem with the 0.7% target

The principle itself beggars belief. It is concerning that there was no economic basis for setting and agreeing an aid target. No simulations were done. The developing world's needs were never assessed. Economists and politicians simply agreed to a figure, in effect a religious tithe by which all rich nations should be bound. The world's development aid target serves no economic purpose. It is a fitting religious ritual. Not that there is anything wrong with borrowing from religious thought to improve mankind's wellbeing where there would be added value. Borrowing from religion has defined most of our development in any case. So that wouldn't be new or unsettling. But you will be forgiven for expecting that economic calculations should be the basis for setting economic targets.

The worship of 0.7% GDP target spend for development aid plays to the suspicion or probability that international development aid is currently not intended or not fit to adequately support the development of any laggards in Africa or elsewhere in the world. But that it might be intended to maintain countries at a level above the drowning line to permit the unhindered flow of global business, placate the psyches of rich countries and operate some savvy PR to unsuspecting citizens and leaders in the world.

The setting of target percentage spends for development aid looks like another failing top – down one lane approach to solving a big problem.

What aid target?

Maybe we should consider a bottom – up approach. The proper way to set development targets is to base it on progress made by beneficiaries. Instead of 'country Northland achieves 0.7% spend on GDP on international development programmes by 2020', how about 'Germany and its partners have Sierra Leone reach a literacy level similar to that in western Europe (90%) within the next 10 years'? Or 'France/United Kingdom or the EU ensure 7 new vocational colleges and 5 new reference hospitals are operational in Northern Nigeria and 48 new high schools, 10 general hospitals and 52 training institutes are operational in Africa's Sahel region within the next 8 years that alongside policy, governance and regulation changes drastically improve the quality of life of 5 million Africans, cut illiteracy by half, and give 120,000 youths the business and vocational skills, confidence and social infrastructure to contribute to the development of their communities'. With these sets of targets, you can then judge which should have a better effect at beating extremism, reducing the marginalization of women and cutting down the number of trans-Sahara or other illegal migrants to Europe.

The problem with the second set of objectives is that it can scare the hell out of unsure politicians who would prefer to sweep the aid envelope under the inattentive feet of their citizenry rather than fight the controversy whether they owe any such duty to developing nations in the first place.

This style of objective setting has benefits but significant setbacks. It might mean development aid use is more transparent and its achievements tangible. All would see when it fails to deliver or what measure of progress it has made. On the other side, it could seem like asking foreign aid to take the place of developing country governments. But in a sense, there is no controversy. Currently, development aid does exactly offer or pretend to take the place of failing governments in several aspects of a country's socio-economic life.

Framing all aid objectives in tangible hardware and software outcomes does not change the thrust of aid. It only makes it easier for the layman donor and beneficiary who have not taken pretentious normative economics courses to actually be able to evaluate aid use. Our aid billions set out to transform Africa's dangerous Sahel region. Where are the 10 general hospitals we set out to make operational? What is the enrolment of the 48 high schools built with our money?

How many girls have escaped early and forced marriage by getting scholarships to the schools we created and our lobbying efforts on governments in the region to apply tough laws on child traffickers? Which regulation changes have we been responsible for? Over the eight years of the programme, how many million Africans were able to improve their economic wellbeing as a result of our intervention? How many new jobs were created by people who took our specialist courses of small business management, obtained a modest loan and invested in income generating activities?

Development planners have hidden some of the really vital metrics by going only for those that despite being certainly useful and frankly difficult to measure appear much easier to manipulate and pass off as near cost free to their taxpayers back home. Made worse because their benefits are only visible to those who are obliged by the profession or drawn by hobby to read such reports. Other important benefits cannot be propagated because of the low visibility of the initial positives. The proceeds, benefits and progress derived from friendly development aid should be visible even to those who don't read UN, World Bank and other international reports. Only through such visibility will development aid be politically and socially sustainable for donor taxpayers.

Of course the visible infrastructure combined with tangible outcomes approach may have its own flaws but they are mostly a matter of prejudice, the absence of political will and a blind reliance on development theories that have continued to fail the donors and supposed beneficiaries. It could be accused of taking the onus for development off the shoulders of African leaders to the afterthought of heads of rich countries. You should expect politicians to blast this off as an attempt to make the rich responsible for the development of other countries. But that is not the case. That's actually far from the truth.

The premise is to ensure that development aid is sufficiently robust and deep to ensure that its impact can be final. Development aid should procure benefits and create shock proof systems for beneficiary communities to be equipped to continually adapt outcomes in order to end the game. It should be in the interest of every genuine politician to bring the rising development aid to an end, a quick end. The need for development aid is a sign of the failure of policy, policy makers, politicians, development planners, leaders, development teaching universities, the United Nations and the several others who have made development their raison d'être.

Aid that is programmed to run indefinitely is a mistake. The first objective of development aid is to end development aid.

It has already been pointed out by too many writers that progress will not sustainably coexist side by side with failure, especially if both are of massive proportions. According to Paul Collier (2007), a future world with impoverished and stagnant countries is just not a scenario we can countenance. A cesspool of misery next to a world of growing prosperity is both terrible for those in the cesspool and dangerous for those who live next to it. We had better do something about it. The question is what.

Will aid encourage Africans to sit back and expect donor countries to develop the continent?

Chapter IV Can Africa be developed from outside?

What we fear doing most is usually what we most need to do – Ralph Waldo Emerson

This is a question that gets asked every now and then. It is a reflection of a certain concern that foreigners or foreign forces are arrogating to themselves the right, the obligation and the resources to develop the countries in Africa. The question is also partly a reflection of the suspicion surrounding foreign attempts to develop Africa, perhaps with solutions devised by the rich West to be imposed on an Africa that is wild, stubborn and slow to learn from the rich.

For many Africans, it is about reconciling with the disturbing wisdom that other people understand Africa more than Africans to be able to judge what forms and speeds of development should suit the continent. For critics, it is whether externally driven development with aid money is a sustainable way of ending the poverty that mires millions of Africans.

Can Africa be developed from outside?

I don't know of any country in the world where a bunch of foreigners came and developed the country. I don't know one: Japan? Korea? No! No country did that. I know about countries that developed on trade and innovation and business. – Herman Chinery-Hesse

There is a saying among the Bantu peoples that goes 'when you go to a funeral, you shouldn't mourn more than the bereaved'. Events over the last two decades have seriously modified the premise of development aid without many taking notice. Aid has been promoted as a tool to develop the world's weakest nations, especially those in Africa. Everything from education, sanitation to environment has been bundled under 'development aid' as in helping poor countries. But if you take a deep look at the unwritten rationale for many aid programmes, you may find they are intended to address problems which if left to their own devices could make their way to developed countries by way of contamination through the global cycle of human interaction and the undeniable fact we are just all part of a single ecosystem.

In today's interconnected world health epidemics in one remote corner, a conflict over diamonds in another and massive soil erosion elsewhere will somehow sometime find a way to affect Europe and America through travel health risk, market price fluctuations for rare minerals and hungry migrants at the shores of the Mediterranean. The recent Ebola Virus Disease epidemic that struck and nearly strangled Sierra Leone, Liberia and Guinea reminded the rich countries of the world how vulnerable they could be to Africa's unsolved development mess.

Can Africa be developed from outside?

We could in the first instance attempt to establish the usefulness of aid.

'Aid does tend to speed up the growth process. A reasonable estimate is that over the past thirty years, it has added around one percentage point to the annual growth rate of the bottom billion[1]. This does not sound like a whole lot, but then the growth rate of the bottom billion over this period has been much less than 1 percent per year-in fact, it has been zero. So adding 1 percent has made the difference between stagnation and severe cumulative decline. Without aid, cumulatively, the countries of the bottom billion would have become much poorer than they are today. Aid has been a holding operation, preventing things from falling apart' Paul Collier in the 'Bottom Billion' (2007).

So aid has been a holding operation. That's one way to see. There are others.

David A. Phillips (2013) quite sensibly disagrees with the view that aid's purported 1% growth rate addition to the economies of recipient poorest economies is anything worth popping champagne on. You have to sympathise with him. Who puts money in a bank to get a 1% return on investment?

It has been estimated that Britain, for instance, has poured more than £1 billion (roughly $1.7 billion) into Ethiopia, Rwanda and Tanzania in a programme ending in 2015 but that despite this effort, a report by the UK's Independent Commission for Aid Impact in 2012 found that basic skills in literacy and math were not improving in the three countries. (Birell, 2014).

One billion British pounds is a tremendous amount of money. Great financial effort by generous taxpayers. Paltry returns. This is just one of perhaps several thousand aid programmes with shipwrecked outcomes. Why and how the programmes failed is another subject. At the very least, someone committed funding to help out a situation. Maybe Paul Collier's argument makes sense here too. Perhaps if the UK had not spent this money to prop up the educational systems in those three countries, basic reading and math skills would have fallen say by 5%. If that is so, therefore in this case, that programme has been a massive success. It may not have met the inflated objectives set out in the beginning to improve literacy by a certain percentage point but it has helped secure the benefits which where earned earlier.

Can Africa be developed from outside?

For what purpose?

The first big question that springs to mind is why. Is development aid fulfilling a moral obligation? Is it an early recognition or suspicion that the world is one body of member countries where diseases affecting some parts eventually find their way to the rest of the organism, with the ability to snuff life out of it? In that case, would global aid not just be a means to serve selfish socio-economic goals in the club of rich donor countries? Why would an outsider want to develop Africa? Is it of any outsider's interest to develop another continent or worse, a disparate agglomeration of countries with multiple identities?

Well, let us assume or in fact agree that people do love foreign lands, even if they are strangers. There are lots of people out there who are so fond of places beyond their national territories that their life's passion is to labour for a better outcome for those distant lands. This however is mostly on a personal plan. Such individual passion for the development of Africa eventually make only a tiny difference, apart from a beautiful tale of bravery, dedication, adventure and friendships with the people. To really develop Africa takes much more. That is what we should contend.

The premise of the possibility of Africa being developed from outside is so wrong it is strenuous to contend for much longer. It is one thing to walk a horse to the spring. It is another to get it drink any water. It may be too simplistic to suggest that Africa does not want to be developed. That would even be outrageous because Africans want it developed more than anyone else. So in principle, the horse is willing to drink. So maybe no one is walking the horse to the stream. Or the stream is so far off the horse does not want to bother. How about the horse walker not agreeing which path to the stream is the shortest and surest?

All honest donors do acknowledge that it is a waste of time and effort to attempt to develop Africa from outside. Donors wish they could show more progress for the billions spent on aid but they can't.

Is it a coincidence that the main development aid contribution target was set at the same time independence and relative sovereignty was dawning on the majority of African countries? Perhaps not. Was the 1% target a moral rent or religious retribution for the theft, exploitation and atrocities that reigned during colonization and thereafter? Was it driven by fear, compassion or guilt? Is it the biggest ever disguised mea culpa?

Can Africa be developed from outside? By whom? To what ends? By which methodology? Attempts at helping Africa develop or supporting the efforts of African governments in developing their countries have at times led to suspicions and accusations on the political sphere. Years of development aid programming with few inspiring success stories has messed the atmosphere. Realisation that development aid interventions should be applied in perhaps more unorthodox ways is beginning to surface.

Another way to look at the question is by peering beyond the geographical dimension. Can Africa be developed from within, using outside ideas, methods, procedures and philosophies? Can the use of experts trained and framed in the operational ideology of the donor, whether these experts are Africans or not, using streams of financial resources packaged and delivered through foreign standards produce significant development?

As things stand, the bulk of development aid is currently programmed through one or a combination of the above strands of development from the outside. The critics who argue that you cannot develop Africa from the outside have clearly won the argument – if there was any argument in the first place. Foreign donors have for long misunderstood Africa, if they intend to develop it from outside. But we can contend that was not the case.

Africa is like a big monster. Its land mass is bigger than all that of its development partners put together. To put things into perspective, Africa is larger than Greece, Bangladesh, Nepal, the United Kingdom, Italy, Norway, Germany, Japan, Sweden, Papua New Guinea, Spain, France, Peru, Mexico, the USA, China and India put together. Africa is not only terribly big, it is frightfully diverse.

Guinea Bissau is not the same as Gabon. Egypt is not the same as Sudan. Zimbabwe is different from Nigeria. Western Sahara is different from Morocco. South Sudan is not nearly similar to Namibia. Tanzania is not even remotely similar to Mali. One country is all desert land (Niger) while another is all forest (Congo). Some African countries are much bigger than their donors. The Central African Republic, CAR, is about one and a half times the size of France. If development means taming the land and channeling the people to produce harmony and economic value that engenders stability and marginal progress, it may be suicidal to imagine France being able to help CAR develop.

Can Africa be developed from outside?
In the first instance, this should not be the question. Let us view it from another angle. Can the US, Europe, Japan, Canada, Australia etc develop themselves by attempting to protect Africa and other developing countries? The nature of some of the development aid propagated by these countries probably suggest the promotion of some mutual benefits. So maybe from now on exit development aid. Here comes global aid.

Global aid

There is a certain realization that the world is only as rich as its poorest nations. In an increasingly globalised world, it is foolhardy to want to access the world's markets while expecting no contamination from its problems. Global aid is here in disguise. Its objective is to mend the bruises apparent in a globalised world and sustain globalization. But you could also argue that these are byproducts of development aid.

The 2015 Ebola Virus Epidemic in West Africa has again reminded us how the strengths or weaknesses of one country constitute a plus or a flaw for the entire world. Guinea, Sierra Leone and Liberia have some of the weakest medical systems on the planet. It seemed their problem alone until Ebola spread to other countries on the African continent, North America and Europe.

Earlier and in a saga that continues in other parts of the world, when the world allowed the Taliban and Al Qaeda to make Afghanistan home and reduce the lives of many to just air to breathe, it wasn't the world's problem until September 11.

The world is such that good and evil cannot be rounded up and confined in a small circle of influence or prosperity. Good and bad developments too are like the molecules in a beaker of water subject to Brownian motion[2]. Left on their own, the kinetic and potential forces of globalization will continuously bombard them until they cross borders to contaminate, dilute or induce the direction of development in other places.

There is a problem with the term 'development aid'. Framing aid as such leads to an omission of rich and middle income countries from the solution as well as the beneficiary chain. It is undeniable that the least developed countries in Africa for example appear to need more aid than the middle income ones in other parts of the world. The term 'development aid' currently biases aid as a drip set needed only by the less developed. But if we changed to call it 'global aid' it could open the door for also tackling the factors in rich countries that accentuate underdevelopment in other parts of the world.

In global aid the world could be dealing with discriminatory trade practices in agriculture and climate change inducing activities for example which contribute to reducing the odds of development for other countries. Global aid will tacitly recognize that the biggest part of aid goes to the rich developed countries. Rather than being in self denial, the world could restructure these reverse flows of aid and drive the massive aid industries in wealthy countries to focus the use of the funds on ending rich country factors that breed the need for development aid elsewhere.

In global aid, there is recognition too that the world is interconnected and failings on one side would eventually find their way to the other side. That might help change the way

[2] Brownian motion is the haphazard movement of molecules in liquids and gases which leads to the molecules spreading out in a given space.

politicians commit funds to addressing global development issues.

The ignorance of the 'experts' who mount television programmes, blot newspaper columns and drink coffee in development policy rooms in rich countries on the true nature of Africa has led Kai Krause to suggest that "In addition to the well known social issues of illiteracy and innumeracy, there also should be such a concept as '*immapancy*', meaning insufficient geographical knowledge. Even if you put all the brains in donor countries and the multitude of multilateral organisations which craft development aid, they will be found wanting on understanding the dynamics of the countries on the continent. In matters of development, there can be no foreign messiahs.

Chapter V What we could change to salvage aid

You can't find new land with old maps.

The frailties of the current aid regime are numerous. The verdict is unflattering. Development aid has not produced as much benefits as everyone had hoped for over the past 50 years, except for a few exceptions. Its successes sound like exceptions. And even in those exceptional cases, the measure of success can be relative. In controlling the spread of HIV/AIDS which is probably the biggest poster child for the success of development aid, it could still be argued that if earlier development aid had been programmed appropriately, there might have been little scope for the virus to take pandemic proportions.

Whilst global aid evangelists would be adamant aid has at least temporarily soothed the wounds of some of the world's suffering, the weight of evidence for those escaping poverty lies in economic growth and not global development aid. That evidence is not cheap. It is overwhelming. How do you teach the poor creativity, innovation and enterprise? That looks like the surest route to murdering poverty. Aid should borrow leaves from what works. But economic development alone does not guarantee that all those trapped near the abyss of human development found in an area of rapid sustained growth will board the bus out of poverty on time.

One of the fallouts from rapid economic growth could be inequality. As the smart, strong, pushy and treacherous take advantage of favourable economic conditions to create wealth for themselves, the rowdiness that exists in such markets usually mean that governments cannot cope with the pace of change. Social safety nets would not yet exist or be properly calibrated to execute effective transfers that could make wealth distribution fairer.

In many places of too rapid economic growth, exploitation of the poor dramatically increases. It gets worse where it involves the exploitation of natural resources where land rights belong to the weak or where the resulting negative externality from the exploitation like pollution, loss of habitat and loss of farmland rather plunges an already impoverished people a few feet further down the poverty drain. Global aid could play a role in supporting fairer income distribution. The global economy is creating global income inequality despite producing growth.

Our way forward

There is scope to consider new ways in which global development aid could be implemented. There are 1.4 billion people living in poverty (as of 2015). The aid worker must be in a haste to finish their mission, pack their bags and go back home in time to drink tea with smug feelings of accomplishment. The experts who run development programmes of wealthy generous governments should tread their office in awe of the poverty figures their children will read rather than bother about their careers and which big job they take on next. The people trapped in poverty do not have the luxury to bother about these things. The poor don't have much time to watch impostors perpetuate the status quo of shame with the very policy approaches which have done nothing other than spurn fabulous figures to them like in a drunkard's dream.

The world needs bold new ways to fructify the investments made via global aid. For an industry that could double to 300 billion dollars annually within the next decade, failure will be a larger embarrassment. One of the blessings or curse in the charity business is that failure has got thick skin. The nobility of its causes coupled with an endless flow of poverty tragedies around the world have provided some insurance to the survival of the aid mechanism, for lack of acceptable workable alternatives. But even the best of luck does not run into infinity. Failure fatigue, a sort of zombie drowsiness born from years of profane waste and a terminal loss of purpose could prove the sector's undoing. The aid scam should not run for much longer.

Cash on delivery and the graduation model

There are recent initiatives judged to hold some promise. These are not yet being applied in great scale but are worth considering in some situations. Cash on delivery (COD) is one of such. It incentivizes the attainment of development objectives by paying some amount of money when a specified target is met. It cannot however be applied to every circumstance. It has helped organisations meet some objectives though. It is too focused on the middleman.

The middleman or aid implementer gets a reward for delivering a service to the poor. The poor is not part of the negotiation.

So, once more, those living in poverty get sidelined by experts and technocrats dispensing the aid loot. It might have been more sensible to have the poor directly pay the 'middleman' for providing them a good service. Cash on delivery is recognition of the deep laxity, inertia and corruption which have rendered many third world public service machinery ineffective in implementing development aid. A risk that the middleman could continuously bargain their cash on delivery commission upwards exists. But where robust systems for measuring outcomes exist, COD is probably better than blind hope on failing governments.

The graduation model for fighting poverty requires five simultaneous interventions in any alleviation package to ensure maximum sustainable success. It establishes that to help a given target person get out of poverty, the target should get: an asset for income generation (1), skills based training to manage the asset (2), primary basic needs like potable water and food to reduce the need for the target to suddenly sell off the income generating asset (3), frequent and regular coaching of the target to reinforce ability and update skills for the target to effectively manage the income generating process in which the asset is employed (4), access to healthcare and health education (5) and a savings scheme to help the target save for rainy days, minimize the temptation to dispose of the asset for fast cash and also potentially invest in other income generating assets. Narrowly focused development aid that attempts to solve problems in isolation does not work. The donor community and in fact all in the global aid industry should surely have discovered this a long time ago.

Where the graduation model strikes a chord is that in one intervention to lift a target population out of poverty, it takes the broad net casting approach. Instead of limiting itself to an income generating activity, in a single programme it delivers health improvement, financial awareness and food security.

The secondary objectives are critically important. They are the levees that protect the primary objective of wealth creation to be safeguarded from loss. They are equally the substrate upon which regeneration and sustainability of the first level objective of income generation rely.

Aid Cornerstones

Aid is necessary and useful. For it to be continuously relevant and useful, it has to remain fair. For aid to be fair, it has to be sustainable. Development aid owes it to taxpayers and contributors in donor countries to be fair. We should ask the question, what should global aid address? For aid to be focused and sustainable, it should be built on three main thematic pillars of health, life skills education and economic infrastructure. This is not to suggest that food relief should be pulled out of the development aid expense heading.

These pillars rather demonstrate that were they to be solidly built, there will be hardly any need for expensive failure signals like food aid in the long run –except in the event of a natural disaster. The majority of aid should be along these three pillars. While some attention is currently paid to health, there is scant focus on life skills education – where in fact, it is this third pillar that has the greatest potential to contribute to the sustainability of aid. Targeting life skills will directly address the biggest concern of people in Africa, for example, where unemployment top their worries.

Aid that doesn't end should not be aid. It should be termed more appropriately a 'human right' or public relations, as applicable. Life skills education can be the main driver of the other minor pillars of development. Economic infrastructure should ensure that there are forums like functional markets and physical factors to enable people trade their skills in services and products.

New Aid Governance

Development aid governance should be reformatted with the following structures and principles to afford it greater accountability, effectiveness and end stakeholder ownership.

i) Public Aid Commission

Donors should be wary of trusting most governments with development money. Governments that perform poorly on corruption perception and other governance indices are bound to 'lose' a good proportion of aid via corruption. It is no mistake that the most corrupt countries tend to peak on the aid recipient charts. While it may be sensible to have a key stakeholder like governments in the management channel of development aid, their limitations have to be recognized and remedied. Over and over, concerned citizens are left baffled at the sums of money that central governments receive or have at their disposal as aid and scant progress that results from its use thereof.

The current model of aid flows bilaterally and multilaterally excludes a significant segment of actors from the control chain. A majority of ODA recipient countries are limping democracies where powerful central governments have crippled all state-run public check and balance systems. This results in aid being unaccounted for, as recipients muddle requests for greater transparency under their umbrella of sovereignty while donors are preoccupied with preparations for the next financial year's budget and attendant pressures to spend money to satisfy budgetary requirements.

Aid suffers a big problem in that at the moment at which it transits from the coffers of the donor to that of the recipient – be it civil society, government or other actor, it is not clear who owns it. Donors soon ignore it – for various perverse reasons, beneficiaries are not aware that they could own it and implementers just sometimes slump over the lack of capacity to use it appropriately.

Every country that receives Overseas Development Assistance should set up an overarching body to monitor, evaluate and propose a steer for aid policy for both donors and recipients. The Public Aid Commission will be a national institution which brings together all the information from bilateral and multilateral donors and monitors aid effectiveness nationwide. Its role will not be to manage aid. It will rather be to aggregate information on programmes, projects, funding streams and monitor performance targets: sustainability, completion, effectiveness, transparency and overall success or failure of official development assistance programmes.

There is not one institution that currently does this, apart from OECD data compilation on spend levels and thematic areas. There isn't country snapshot of aid use that provides a clear picture of where aid money has gone to, the details of progress it has affected, its shortcomings and the gaps it was not able to fill. This could be an important improvement on aid governance. The technology is available. Donors, African governments, aid agencies and civil society need to be creative about improving visibility of progress made through development aid.

Some ministerial departments in certain countries are attempting to gather this information. But their purpose is significantly different from what is mentioned here. In one country, the ministry of economy is trying to find out how much each donor pumps into the country annually and in which sectors. That's just the problem. Aid as a number. That's what these economic planners focus on. A number. A sector. A numeric goal. Not a quality, a deliverable or an accomplishment. All they want is to feed in the figures into economic planning and inflate GDP and ODA. We couldn't be misleading ourselves more. Aid spend figures are among some of the most misleading pieces of information. Development aid should as a matter of principle be quoted in deliverables, achievements, changes effected, verified outcomes and objectives met and not in dollar amounts.

The Commission should not be a government department. It should be composed of government representatives, civil society, donors and representatives of beneficiaries. This is one way of ensuring corrupt governments do not go unnoticed and unquestioned for aid use. It will cover all aid use, including that by civil society. The Public Aid Commission would make recommendations on improving the implementation of aid, checking fairness and sounding alarm bells when whole regions are marginalized and deprived from development like the northern halves of Cameroon and Nigeria. The commission should be the combined custodian of development aid money. The commission could use various tools for monitoring and stakeholder engagement including non-traditional ones like Community Audits for Transparency and Accountability, CATA.

CATA is a method of non-legal supervision and monitoring of public funds use which deviates from technical principles of accounting and audit in that it uses a periodic community conference (quarterly for instance) where local council officials appear before citizens of their community to explain how money has been used. Civil society organizations would have prepared themselves and communities for budget monitoring beforehand. During the community audit, when the council or mayor says 'we have constructed a given number of water taps – for example, community members will ask the authorities to name the locations. The people can then directly confirm whether this is true or not and discuss any issues they have with the project, asking about the cost of each one and who the contractor was.

In one such Community Audit for Transparency and Accountability which was organized, 10 taps announced by the mayor turned out to be 6 confirmed by the community and to the embarrassment of the mayor, he was not even aware that his technical services had failed to deliver the other four. The council authorities also learnt that an abandoned and dilapidated health centre they were planning to refurbish would not be used by the community because it lay on the site of historic tribal fights for boundary land.

While there was peace and the law court had long established who owned the land, people preferred to avoid the area, fearing spiritual reprisals from those who had lost – and this consciousness had spread among the people. No one was willing to trust any life-saving service found along the old disputed territory.

The community audit turned out to be an enabler of democracy and responsible governance without the costs of legal proceedings and audit missions just by the local government realizing that people were watching and there would be community consequences. Such a control mechanism chimes well with the dispositions of many African communities as it mirrors the continent's original democracy.

ii) Access to Information

Countries receiving development aid must be made to enact access to information laws to promote civil society and local citizenry's ability to scrutinize, question and contribute ideas to the use of aid money. Promulgating an access to information bill that effectively covers such public financial transactions should be a condition sine qua non for becoming a country benefitting from aid. It is unbelievable that donors are still wasting their citizens' money in countries where the public cannot legally ask what has become of the funds.

It must not stop in the statute books. There are rigorous conditions to be met to become an EU member country, a member of NATO and to gain EITI compliant status. But the most common rigours around receiving aid tend to have been in writing complicated technical bids for project money. Active transparency – not passive - should be embedded in the complete cycle of development aid distribution agenda.

Development aid like any other aid for that matter should not be complicated. The complications in administering aid favour the growth of a bureaucracy that knows how to beat the system. Is it asking too much to ask all countries that receive development aid to regularly publish the accounts of aid money? Should the price of a packet of pencils not be made public? Should governments be allowed under the guise of sovereignty not to give full disclosure on the use of aid money?

Admittedly, there are certain types of development projects for which too much publicity could scupper any benefits they might be hoping to create. But these projects constitute a tiny minority of development aid.

Access to information is a critical ingredient for an effective development aid regime. This must go beyond the reporting requirements to donors. Aid information should be a matter of public interest. There must be an equal if not higher obligation to report aid transparently to the public. Most countries are ill equipped for this both legally and operationally. Government officials and aid contractors can find several excuses for not having or being able to disclose the complete set of information for development aid use.

The way to go is to step run faster than the legal loopholes. It could take a long time to get parliaments to sit, study and agree access to information laws. Not because these are difficult to do but because of rotten politics, bad governance and a fear of anything prejudiced with the 'western' tag. Some African countries like Nigeria already have an access to information law. But this shortcoming can be overcome.

Development aid planners should insist on a disclosure section being part and parcel of any bid documentation. The disclosure section should carry clear reporting requirements which proactively set the responsibility for proof of transparency on the recipient so that implementers should embed in their plans public reporting through more media: online, print, sign posting, public explanation, responding to mails or others.

African Civil Society

Many western donors and their development agencies have a terrible attitude towards African civil society. They pay lip service. They bash governments for reducing civil society space. They criticize the frailties if not overall absence of strong indigenous civil society in African countries. A lot of this criticism may be justified. But that is not the issue. The question is: who should be helping civil society in Africa? To rescue development aid and render it more effective, African civil society must be strengthened and empowered with the right level of funding and human resources to adequately support the development process.

End discriminatory funding. We don't fund this, … we don't fund that, … . But western civil society gets funds for operational expenses and seed money most of the time. We have to realize that African CSOs do not have seed money.

Rich donors, instead of resolving the imbalance tend to treat them like beggars. The unfortunate effect is that the global development aid industry is tilted to the advantage of donor countries. Aid ends up with the 'big' organisations, well funded, well staffed by old and 'new' citizens of developed countries and with a larger percentage of financial flows from aid returning to banks in first world countries.

Be partners with African indigenous CSOs and not unruly competitors. To be fair, there are sparks of partnership and collaboration between International Non Governmental Organisations and local ones. That's usually when a donor imposes such partnership as a condition for money to trickle through the accounts of the developed country-based INGO. What should stop is the big brother attitude. Several local NGOs just need to be empowered with the trust, training and funding needed to reach their full levels of performance.

Civil society organisations perhaps suffer their biggest rivalry from government departments. But even government departments are apt to run to CSOs as the last resort to effect meaningful progress in the community. Many African governments have now accepted some of the civil society pills the West or more appropriately realities on the ground has forced down their throats. But this is mostly in non contentious sectors of the country's development. Foreign donor, recipient governments and international organisations should see local civil society organisations and activists as their best assets in the race for development and not like a group of street children whose undisclosed morality gets you running for shelter.

Local civil society needs money to hire and retain qualified staff, keep them in a proper office and give them a reason to build a career focused on delivering progress in their communities. Low staff quality in the milieu will continuously ensure aid delivers little or nothing. With low staff quality and integrity, the lone beneficiary of aid money would most times be the manager/founder of the organization who will find no opposition in redirecting the aid money to some personal investments in real estate. The presence of high quality staff in local organisations is an important deterrent for rampant misappropriation of funds.

Reciprocate aid

There is no reason why third world countries cannot give development aid to 'wealthy' developed nations. For nearly half a century, we have witnessed the flow of development money from one source (developed countries) to two groups of recipients: developing countries on the one hand and to themselves (developed countries) through an intricate kickback mechanism discussed earlier in this book. The doctrine and tradition that aid flows in only one direction from wealthy countries to poorer ones is immoral. That the United States of America, France, Belgium, the United Kingdom or any other European country can plough billions of dollars into Nigeria, Cameroon, Ghana, Senegal, DR Congo, Kenya and others year in, year out creates an unhealthy subordinate complex between giver and taker. This subordinate complex distorts all the trade deals which giver and taker negotiate in one side's favour.

It is very easy to deny the existence of a subordinate complex. It is designed to be so. It is subtle and immaterial. This complex is born from a fallacy that assumes that wealthy countries are doing okay and have a swell time while third world ones are cursed on the majority with looting dictators, despots and broken systems.

Countries do not need to be declared wealthy or developed in order to give aid. To their credit, either as part of a saintly mission or a cunning scheme, developed countries have gone out of their way to de-prioritise or simply ignore some of their own problems to put money in global development aid. It is wrong for countries to receive and receive aid and give back nothing in return. The giving of aid is not conditional upon a country solving all of its own home-based problems. Aid is a solidarity cause between friendly nations. Others have deformed it into a tool of control, distraction and appeasement.

Aid should return to the spirit of solidarity. Reciprocating aid will be a humbling and learning process for both recipients and donors. Should America refuse to collect aid from Ghana, the African country should be suspicious and immediately terminate all programmes for aid acceptance with Washington. Reciprocating aid is not expensive and out of reach. The amount does not matter. It is the principle that counts. African countries can afford to reciprocate aid. Do not forget that third world countries lose more money through corruption than they get from development aid. If developing countries cut corruption by just 10%, they will be in a position to help the European Union, the USA and Japan with some 20 billion dollars to alleviate some of the socio-economic problems affecting rich nations.

Reciprocating aid works on the premise that every country, no matter how destitute media may paint it, how despotic its leaders, and how broken its infrastructure, still has an area of unique competitive advantage such that it can lend a helping hand to others. Even if such competitive advantage were not to exist, as a matter of dignity and in line with the principle of equality among nations – with none being subservient to the other, reciprocating aid would be the imperative line of action. You do not need to be wealthy and basking in plenty to help your friend. You just need to have a discerning spirit to see that they need help, the heart to feel for them and the will to share your love and concern.

All 24 member countries of the Development Aid Committee (DAC) of the Organisation for Economic Cooperation and Development have problems which even their own sometimes relatively robust political and economic systems have failed to tame. The model of development aid sculpted on so called wealthy nations donating money to so called poor ones has been a costly moral error, a political misdemeanour and an economic gaffe thriving on the gullibility of third world countries and their inability to see the hidden intricate systems connecting development support and neo-colonial domination.

By accident or by design, aid has too easily worked in favour of the donor as if literally reaping the prophetic rewards of the Holy Bible's *'It is more blessed to give than to receive'* precept. One of the clear ways we could test the sincerity of purpose of this model is to employ the reciprocation of aid.

Britain is unable to adequately staff its health system, even after hijacking medical talent from several developing countries, especially the Philippines. France, the US and much of Europe are in a similar situation. But the United Kingdom, France, the US and the EU all give aid to 'poor' countries. The US has three million homeless people. The number of homeless in America exceeds the population of two African countries together: Gabon and Equatorial Guinea. But America manages to give out billions in foreign aid.

Juvenile delinquency in France reached such heights over the 2005 – 2015 decade that the country's governments have at times feared for their own survival and their much acclaimed social stability. Religious intolerance is so high in France that hardly a month goes by without a flashpoint, a desecration or a politically incorrect declaration in the media to illustrate the malaise or the rot affecting 'la fraternité'. France still issued development aid throughout these dark periods.

In Spain, unemployment reached 40% at one point after the global financial crisis of 2008. Madrid did not end its international development programme. Being a wealthy country is not a prerequisite for giving foreign aid. African countries and other third world nations in Asia as well as middle income ones can and should give global development aid to the 'rich' West.

The OECD's Development Assistance Committee member countries who issue the bulk of development aid have problems of their own. According to Transparency International's Corruption Perception Index in 2012, Greece at 94th looks terribly corrupt, its economy tumbling ever since; South Korea has a shocking suicide rate; the United States has a gun homicide rate that makes many failed states feel like paradise; in 2007, a report by Privacy International cited key DAC member as countries with such an extensive government surveillance that they are akin to third world dictatorships, … just to mention a few. All countries have big problems, whether rich or poor. As no country has zero per capita income, every country in the world should be able to give some development aid to any country in the world.

America has problems, big problems of its own. Bush I was not able to fix it. Clinton I was not able to fix it. Bush II was not able to fix it. Obama failed to fix it. The next president will not fix it. The problem: rising cost of university education and its attendant unbearable student debt. In the US, the average cost of tuition and fees for the 2014–2015 school year was $31,231 at private colleges, $9,139 for state residents at public colleges, and $22,958 for out-of-state residents attending public universities. With room and board, the figures double to $62,000 per year at private colleges, $19,000 for state residents at public institutions and $45,000 for out-of-state residents attending public universities.

The average tuition and fees for a university student in a public university in Cameroon is under $400 per annum. Including living costs per year it gets to $2,400. It is over fifteen times more expensive to earn an undergraduate degree in the US than at a good publicly funded university in a stable African country. Cost wise, there's no reason why a few Americans cannot be given 'free' education in Cameroon and in several other developing countries annually. But education is not just about money. There are other considerations. Let us consider the quality of education.

It is important to do this because western journalists with a sense of geography stretching no further than their daily commute for work have deceived unsuspecting inhabitants of first world countries that Africa is desperately wretched in all respects. The top 200 universities in Africa are arguably as good as or better than the bottom half of universities in the United States, especially when it comes to fields not requiring heavy investment in science, technology and research. American education is great – no doubt. But that could be a misleading conclusion.

More appropriately, the excellent US universities are really outstanding and world pacesetters. But there are about 4,000 universities in America. They are not all great. They are not all good. By American users' own acknowledgement, some are outright crap, mediocre and an absolute waste of money. Hundreds of US universities and community colleges will not make the grade in the league of Africa's big 200. And the top performing universities in developing countries will usually be three to twenty times cheaper than the ones in America. So in terms of cost and quality, several African countries hold a nominal competitive advantage in undergraduate education over the USA. This would also be true for several humanities and social science postgraduate degrees.

Admittedly, African universities will struggle in the high end advanced sciences and technology. This is only so because these departments require hefty funding packages, big investments and infrastructure to attract grey matter and more research money to plug themselves usefully in a country's economic development chain. Even in the US, only a small fraction of universities are in that league. Not every student in America wants to go to college to build the technology that plots mankind's invasion of space. Not everyone will be reading nano technology or advanced nuclear physics. That leaves the hordes that flock into humanities, the arts and social sciences for a fair bit of college education in Africa, at no debt – crucially.

African universities have their vices. But they are not all broken. Even within the half broken ones, they world has managed to reap some of the best scientists, writers, thinkers, statesmen, professors and pacesetters of global repute. Thousands of students graduating with degrees from countries in African countries that receive aid from OECD countries are scoring top marks in courses at America's universities. Some end up as faculty there and leaders in business and society.

We have skipped over the cost and quality hurdles. Let us get to the crux of the action. Third world African countries should be helping a few thousand American students graduate without debt. There is no reason why American students should not take a scholarship opportunity to study in an African university. Such scholarships will help several thousand US citizens escape the violence, poverty and social exclusion that plaque their communities. It will increase American understanding of the world beyond Mexico, China and Paris. This will be a powerful contribution to the dialogue of cultures that promotes world peace and harmony between peoples and nations.

Almost all developing countries are able to offer a minimum of 100 university level scholarships to citizens of foreign aid donor countries. There are over half a dozen in Africa which can sustainably offer up to a thousand such scholarships. These new graduates will modify their countries' perceptions of Africa, in particular and their future influence could be instrumental in changing levels of bias and injustice towards developing countries in the jungle of international affairs.

Africa needs new friends. Developing countries can actually groom their own friends and this will not cost them their teeth and tongue. As well as being development aid, scholarships are trade promotion tools.

Resolve donor country injustices

Citizens of developing countries who ironically should be receiving development aid support are being discriminated against by policies of the same donor countries that intend to 'help' the third world develop. The United States, Canada, the United Kingdom, Australian and others charge a higher tuition fee for anyone from a poor country who wants to attend university abroad. Sometimes the fee differential can be as high as double the standard fee. So in effect, poor students from Africa and Asia are subsidizing the education of Americans, Canadians, the British and Australians.

Instead of OECD DAC countries preoccupying themselves in transferring funds via programmes to poor countries as foreign aid, it may be more responsive to the needs of developing countries for the tuition fees discrimination to end and international levies scraped for citizens of DAC ODA recipient countries who further their education in universities in rich donor countries. That will permit more people to acquire the education and skills necessary to help themselves and their communities escape poverty.

Wholesome or Lifetime Aid

This is not to suggest aid should go on forever. If that were the case, the purpose and equity for aid would have been defeated. Aid should have a definite time span. But effective aid needs enough time for impact. Tying aid programmes to the one to three year cycle has not yielded much success. It takes six years to complete elementary education, six to seven years for secondary and 3-4 years for a first degree. It takes 3-4 years to on average to become professionally skilled in a trade or other endeavour. Economists have estimated that most sub Saharan African countries need economic growth rates of 9% minimum for at least 7 years in a row for a significant proportion of their inhabitants to emerge from poverty. It is sensible to conclude that the thousands of aid programmes that are less than three years in duration will have little or no impact whatsoever on the economic growth of beneficiary countries.

Development aid has too often been brief, tied to a donor or recipient's financial cycle or political calendars which only men and institutions adhere to. Poverty, malnutrition and poor health don't read those calendars. Those ills pay no allegiance to anyone's programme time charts. Usually and barring cases of sudden natural catastrophe, poverty has taken decades to install itself comfortably in the fabric of communities. Famine has arrived after cycles of erosion, poor yield, failed agricultural policy, disease and climate change have taken their toll on the environment. For policy makers to think these ills can go away in stunt type 12, 24 or 36 month programmes is a serious misjudgment.

The solution could lie in wholesome or lifetime aid. This aid model considers both the duration and the breadth of the aid programme. This refers to aid programmes being run for at least the minimum duration for effectiveness at full resources which is reckoned to be 6 to 7 years for most poverty alleviation, education for livelihood, health and food security programmes. It is necessary to get policy makers to delink funding programmes from political cycles of power for this to work.

The other tenet of wholesome/lifetime aid is the breadth of coverage. Aid should cover the three cornerstones identified earlier (health, life skills education and economic infrastructure). It makes little sense, when targeting a community with aid which is threatened by malnutrition as a result of failed crops due to a harsh environment, to focus the aid entirely on bags of rice and environmental improvement.

The health element will manage any disease outbreaks and ensures a strong workforce is available to take to the farms. The life skills education module will shed light on other opportunities for the community to adapt and solve their problems themselves and in economically viable ways.

Currently, most donors' funds are structured to target only one theme. Without a synchronized aid programmed to support the other pillars, the nutrition/environment only approach will lead to unsustainable results. Donors and development planners should structure their funding programmes using wholesome/lifetime aid for effectiveness and sustainability. Brief monothematic aid programmes leave huge development gaps.

Every year since 2005, a major news outlet in the West runs an article that contemplates results of research pointing that development aid was harming Africa rather than helping it. Don't take this an attempt by selfish Europeans to deny help to Africa. It is necessary to look at the argument carefully. This appears to be an interesting research finding. Its shocking and controversial finding makes it even more relevant for serious consideration in the aid debate as we attempt to find ways of making development aid more effective.

There is a puzzling research conducted on households in five villages in countries in Africa. It investigated the impact of new, potable water taps to rural communities suffering from water hygiene problems. The creation of water taps with aid money apparently led to family sizes getting larger. Surely due to the increased health benefits of drinking safer water in ready and plentiful quantity.

The knock-on effect was that as family size increased, young people left the villages to urban locations in search for jobs, better opportunities for living and the city life. This obviously leads to another knock on effect. In 2050, over 60% of Africa's 2 billion people could be squatting in cities. And so as the young people converged on cities, half decent city resources became even more broken. Unable to cope with increased demand for services, health facilities, housing and sanitation, quality of life in the cities slumped, surely creating large ugly slums as dreams of a better life vaporised into a toxic social mess of violent crime, rape, garbage mountains, juvenile delinquency and adult hopelessness.

There might have been other aggravating circumstances in the sample population. It would be faint to attribute an increased family size to the availability of new potable water taps alone. Did the closeness of the taps to homes now mean women were less busy, less occupied and more available for the business of reproduction? In some villages, women get up as early as 4:00 in the chilling morning cold to start the long trek for water. If the presence of water taps now meant they could be in bed till seven in the morning; that should have consequences on family size.

Many couples tend to meet between around the fourth and fifth hour of the morning when their bodies are well rested from the previous day's troubles. Was there any event that affected fertility or the age at which girls started engaging in sex? Was there a religious incentive promoted by a local church? Was there an unsubstantiated fear among the people that diseases could wipe out their offspring and so they were better off making more? Did the water supply project coincide with an influx of male migrants into those communities? Were there any announcements of huge projects in the city by governments which sucked away the youths and led to couples wanting to replace them to avoid an empty nest?

Did a health and health education breakthrough reduce maternal and infant mortality? Did the taps coincide with a change in local attitudes and cultural shift in the definition of ideal family size? Were local conflicts or anxieties about potential ones and their feared consequences on village manpower and land occupation at work in the minds of families? Did families see the abundant potable water supply as an opportunity to increase family manpower, which is something perhaps they had always wanted to do?

Lots of other adjoining issues could have affected the birth rate and flow of youths from potable drinking water communities going off to cities to join the urban mess. But nevertheless, the results of the research should still be an eye opener.

An article in the UK's Telegraph newspaper reporting the findings of the report to the British audience was titled 'Development Aid might be harming Africa'. First, this suspicion is a misrepresentation of development aid. The fact that the taps where funded from development aid money is irrelevant. They could have been funded from local taxes, government investment funds or by some individuals and community organisations who bother about the wellbeing of people in their community. And the outcome knock on effects would have been identical. So aid money cannot be held up like the culprit here. Development aid money is just money. It hasn't got a different coloration from other sources of income for development projects in Africa. It doesn't smell any differently. *A rose, by any other name will smell as sweet.* But what can the findings of this research teach us?

Wholesome development aid could be the way to go. Patchwork aid like the potable water taps above doesn't deliver lasting benefits, as illustrated above, despite their façade. In fact, some of their after effects under certain conditions could compound other development problems. The outcomes could have been a lot different if the aid above was comprehensive and wholesome.

If they had combined this water supply project with a rigourous education on family planning, some sensitization on the hidden realities of city life and a rural livelihood training and support programme to develop the rural economy, the youths wouldn't have thronged to the city to multiply its woes. The reverse could have been possible instead. It is important for development aid donors and policy makers to realize that their good deeds might actually create bigger problems than they solve. Half-hearted, half-baked, shortsighted aid will only perpetuate the need for aid and sustain an industry that survives most times on perhaps unintended but perverse incentives.

Lifetime/wholesome aid would ask the question, what would happen to the families who now have access to abundant good quality water 15 years from this project? If this project has positive and negative knock on effects, where and how best should we channel these effects in order to be able to manage them properly? Could we use this project to extract people from the slums in the bubbling cities to the rural areas and accompany it with additional measures to balance off the development? Unless development aid is comprehensive, there will always be research like this, with findings that rightly mock the purpose of development aid.

The people who run such research and those that hold up their dismal results should not be simply dismissed as doomsday prophets of aid, haters of a suffering Africa, racially motivated political activists or other dirty word. It might be necessary to reason with them that even development aid is subject to the rule of diminishing returns. Theirs may be an attempt to find that point where the positive proceeds from aid turn to a kind of witchcraft that destroys other development gains achieved through hard work over the years. And we can contend that some aid could potentially become witchcraft by design or omission especially when it is severely narrow-minded as most aid currently dispensed in the developing world.

Go to Nigeria's enclaved communities, mourn their lack of access roads. Build the roads of disenclavement to potentially let the people have access to market roads for their produce. Do just that. Don't do any properly equipped and permanently staffed health centres in the formerly enclaved areas. Don't do any vocational training schools for youth. Ignore injustice in land ownership and labour practices. Ignore water too. Well, you may have just compounded Lagos's population problems. The youths in the community will soon learn the sweet smelling one-sided success tales of large sprawling urban centres.

Rumour will fool them that they can have more than roads in Lagos. They can have schools, health facilities, all sorts of mineral water and opportunities for work. They can have a cultural life and a night life. They will think they can see and even touch the stars, rub shoulders with moguls, corporate and global thugs in smooth jackets. They will also have learnt that life doesn't start and end with good roads. One also needs good broadband internet and proper telephone network coverage. The result? They'll take the road that was just built to disenclave their community and hit … you guessed right … the sprawling slums of misery, crime and inhumanity in Lagos. Narrow-minded development could have witchcraft effects like these.

Aid Direct and Shadow Money

The world has witnessed an unprecedented rapid development of new technologies. New tech is drastically changing the way the world does business, the way people interact and the way we learn among countless other changes. Information and communication technology has not been employed nearly enough in administering aid. ICT should play a pre-eminent role in aid governance. While there are a few laudable initiatives taking some innovative engagement systems to underdeveloped communities, the use of ICTs as a vehicle for aid has been scant.

One of the biggest reasons for the failure and low impact achievement of past and current aid programmes has been down to the middleman. It can prove difficult or frightful to circle the aid middlemen as vectors of failure because of their pivotal role in the aid chain. Who are aid's middlemen?

It is fair to recognize that without the brokerage, advocacy skills and availability for field deployment of middlemen like the UN system, several international non-governmental organizations, local NGOs and various civil society organizations, what is today development aid could have been lying uncomfortably in coffers where they are not in absolute necessity. However, the nature of some middlemen with their high maintenance lifestyle, corruption and some carlessness constitute a significant link of inefficiency in the development aid chain.

Aid Direct is simple. It simply recognizes that the advanced technologies available in our world today should alter the role of middlemen, eliminating them altogether in certain aid scenarios. Aid Direct proposes that the middlemen- fat organizations – make way for technology to become the primary medium for the transactions between the donor and the recipient. Money will be saved and the savings can be converted to increased aid for more beneficiaries or greater assistance to beneficiaries. While it may not be feasible to eliminate the middlemen in all cases altogether, it should be possible in many scenarios to limit their role to preparing beneficiaries to link up to donor facilities.

In a brief example, let's say a village in Sudan, where maternal mortality is high, parents are unwilling to send female children to school- paying fees and buying books can't be their priority as there is a famine forecast in the region. The women stay at home because they lack capital to do any business. Currently available technology is able to ensure that if 120 women in one such community would be aided with USD 100 each; they could use predefined quotas of their aid allocation for the following: fees for two children $20, small business loan $50, seeds for planting $15 and health visits $15. USD 12,000 is about the maintenance costs of a typical international staff for one month. It happens to be the same amount needed by 120 women to have a good year in a troubled country. See what difference it could make to the lives of women in an entire community.

The current middlemen and governments should now be focusing their efforts on building the ecosystem for Aid Direct including the various service points of sale for targeted communities, profiling of aid targets, audit mechanism and ensure that the system is cash-free or robust, even if cash is used. Money only circulates electronically – via mobile phones and a new bank card system. Kenya has proven inclusion and large scale coverage with its mobile money systems. Nigeria's e-identity card with embedded bank card chips is another pointer to this being possible at no significant additional cost. DAC-listed countries just need to develop partnerships with card makers for an improved version of national identity cards that could serve several other health purposes including medical information and direct aid consumption.

End budget support to governments of underdeveloped countries

One of the big criticisms leveled against aid is its distortion of growth, its poisonous effect on democracy and its dependency inducing effect on supposed poor beneficiaries. But as with others, these imperfections can be smoothened away. We have already seen that what has succeeded in lifting millions of people out of extreme poverty is economic growth. Our challenge is to get aid to mimic economic growth.

Aid distorts the power dynamics in both donor and recipient countries. In donor countries, the government which collects taxes from its citizens and charities that take donations from supporters of causes over time develop a kind of moral superiority and power complex over these same tax payers and contributors. Governments, aid agencies and charities subject their 'contributors' to a constant bombardment of their psyches and use subtle guilt-bullying techniques and godlike pretentions to extract even more money from the people. On the receiving end, a similar framework operates for what looks like a morality guilt pyramid scheme.

An aid recipient government or a clique of people who receive money on behalf of the impoverished masses with a less than satisfactory governance record pervert the already fractured purpose of aid to lord it over the weak and poor. You are keeping the poor's money. The poor have elected you to office or for NGOs, the poor have accepted your imposture to fend for their wellbeing. Now you have the money which the poor did not give to you. De facto, it is now your money. The poor must now lick your boots to have a meal with the money you received from foreign aid in favour of these same poor. You can use aid money to earn votes using politically targeted projects or wrongfully and shamelessly claiming the political dividends for a new tap, a well, a new school block or batch of generic drugs. Democracy is killed in cold blood.

Shadow money could help reform the power dynamics and return some level of control to the people. In shadow money, rich donor country governments and organisations donate their funds virtually directly to the millions who need it – the people in poverty. The money remains literally virtual. It can only be used to buy bundles of goods meeting a range of pre-defined needs. The recipient cannot actually make a cash withdrawal – (except the particular shadow money programme allows for a small percentage of cashable allocations to be used without tethering).

Shadow money holders can only elect to use part or all of their global aid funds on pre-agreed priorities. Governments collect taxes on shadow money transactions as they would from any other commercial exchange. But the government only gets paid this tax, say for example 15%, after the economic agent (the poor who received global aid in the form of shadow money) spends the money. The tax which governments thus receive should replace the free cash injections governments in underdeveloped countries receive as part of global development aid.

Power and dignity thus returns to the people. They understand that they are paying their taxes. They are taking part in business transactions. Governments rely on them for tax returns. They can withhold tax by refusing to trade. Careless governments will have an incentive to work for the interest of the money. Aid money would suddenly find more than a custodian. It gets an 'owner' who can call the shots. In this arrangement, governments could be serving their people, instead of being sounding boxes for foreign interests during the times when it is not their unique personal profits they are seeking.

If donated amounts do not result to a 'business transaction' within a specified time frame, which could be anything from three months to one full financial year, or even three years, the money defaults back to the original donor. Recipients can empower both themselves and their governments by engaging in approved transactions. Crucially, a democratic principle can be sustained. The people can have a measure of power to control and constrain the actions of those they place in power. They can weaken their governments by refusing to trade in shadow money ventures. Governments will thereby get an additional incentive to demonstrate proper use of aid tax money.

The next big issue to resolve in this formula is the question of priorities. Setting priorities needs a thorough makeover. Several donors are currently serving 'their' own priorities and these are not necessarily priorities of the beneficiaries. A recent study by Afrobarometer (2015) found the following to be the most important problems of Africans: unemployment, health, education and infrastructure in that order. The study further discovered that priorities varied significantly from one country to the other. While in Burkina Faso and Guinea the biggest source of concern was water supply, in Kenya and Madagascar, it was crime and insecurity. Poverty was the biggest problem in Burundi while Algeria was the only country where housing appears to be a massive issue. Rather than dismiss poverty as a big concern, the report buttresses the point that Africans see employment as the golden route to solving their problems. It does a great job of helping global aid donors to Africa figure out what matters to the people and what doesn't.

If donors set priorities which do not appeal to or chime with the needs of the people, they will not trade and the donor money should remain in the vault until donors consult beneficiaries appropriately to arrive at objectives that chime most with recipient's needs. Donors should as far as possible not be in the business of setting priorities for beneficiaries. In the world of global development aid, songs like 'he who pays the piper calls the tune' don't play. That won't work. The donor should seek to understand the priorities of recipients and work to support them in achieving the latter's aims. In development aid, it is the dancer who calls the tune. If this is not so, he who pays would have wasted their money.

What could be the consequence of a shadow money aid programme? Third world countries will be faced with stark choices. Aid recipient countries whose governments operate a rogue governance system based on all forms of corruption could feel threatened. The façades of democracy running in most of these conflict and emergency prone countries could face a test so stern it could be a turning point in the history of the country. Shadow money will end the need of any direct aid to a country's government, which is currently the way most aid works. Governments will now be faced with a different kind of citizen. One who has a vote that can no longer be bought for two dollars at an election and also holds the financial vote (in taxes) which government relies on to operate. With the prospect of laying filthy hands on cheap money from foreign aid becoming a little complicated by the shadow money programme, the necessity of change will be apparent to all as the only route to survival.

How would change come? What kind of change is possible? Illegitimate governments will accuse the rich West donor international community of subversion. They could see the shadow money enterprise as Western efforts to overthrow their governments. The potential for shadow money to restore a reasonable level of democracy could lead to the beneficiary country suspending the cooperation programme altogether. Even so, their masks would have already fallen for all to see.

However, other governments will seize the opportunity to promote a reformist agenda. They will come from the point of view that every government whose citizens have money to spend should start celebrating its economic success. They will raise their economic ambitions from targeting growth rates of 6% to gunning for 10%. They will be keen to leverage the new found economic freedom of some of their poorest to provide the infrastructure that makes their spending possible. This will include schools, health centres and roads in difficult to access parts of the country. The government could feel the imperative to directly work for citizen chosen priorities rather than diktats from bilateral and multilateral development partners.

The idea of giving money directly to people to help them manage a critical turn in their lives is not new. The paradox is that the countries that flout their development aid contributions use this approach in dealing with situations where their citizens face crisis of all sorts: disaster, environmental catastrophe, growing poverty in times of economic slowdown and also to boost spending when economies are gloomy. Following the 2009 Economic Recovery Act, Barack Obama's government issued cash payments to households. No questions were asked as to the nature of expenses beneficiaries will be putting the funds to.

After floods hit parts of the United Kingdom in January 2016, the government set up plans to put substantial sums of money into the hands of victims. There was cash for personal expenses, cash to rebuild damaged houses and further cash to re-finance small businesses.

Notice how they did not give seminars on citizenship, training on the importance of environmental planning, symposia on the rights of tenants during a natural disaster, workshops on disaster policymaking and regional conferences on storm resistant construction. Governments went straight into the crux of the matter to alleviate the sufferings of the people with cash injections while public bodies in back office work drew lessons from the catastrophe and charted policy responses to face future threats.

You could argue that the victims were getting taxpayers' money from their governments. In other words, they were getting their money back. Taxpayers' money. The only problem with this defence is that even the billions of dollars which rich country governments spend in the development aid black hole is also called taxpayers' money. One pill doesn't work for the rich and another for the poor. If the poverty-trapped individuals in wealthy countries can be given cash to help them get out of poverty, the destitute poor in third world countries would not mind the same treatment. Cash is good and cash is good for everyone.

Instruments - Health Balance Exchange

As more and more qualified health workers are caught up in the dragnet from developing countries to feed the health super consumers of developed nations in the West and Northern Hemisphere, the world's health gap has little chance of narrowing between the two. It is no surprise that on the UN Human Development Index, the majority of African countries find themselves between 145 and 187, the low human development bracket. Rich countries with ageing populations and stronger purchasing power are attracting qualified labour from poorer countries which tend to have greater primary healthcare needs. Thousands of foreign nurses constitute the backbone of the NHS in the United Kingdom. In 2012, a report read on Radio France Internationale warned that there are more medical doctors of Beninese origin living in one French city alone, Paris, than in the whole of Benin itself. This drain of medical grey matter is causing havoc in poorer countries.

Statistics from the Health and Social Care Information Centre (HSCIC) in the UK (2014) showed that 11% of all staff who work for the UK's National Health Service (NHS) and community health services are not British. For professionally qualified clinical staff, that rate rises to 14%. For doctors, it gets to 26%. The UK's health manpower uses staff from at least 108 countries with developing nations India, Philippines, Nigeria, Zimbabwe and Pakistan among the top 10 contributors. These stats do not include GPs.

The USA and Canada among others also have foreigner doctor figures well in excess of 24% of the workforce in that profession.

It is costly to train highly specialized medical professionals. Most of them spend 6 to 7 years in basic education, 6 to 7 in secondary, and 4 to 7 in post secondary medical training depending on their field – bio-chemistry, nursing, laboratory, general medicine or in a specialism. Most of this is funded publicly or subsidized in great part by public funds. Yes, funded by taxpayers' money in low income countries, the same countries global organizations are 'helping' to fight poverty. Most of this investment is 'lost' to wealthier nations – Canada, USA, UK, France, Australia, etc who have no caps on how much talent they can recruit each year but have either placed caps on what percentage of their GDP can go to development aid or are monitoring the figures with miser-like caution.

A fraction of aid to developing countries is eventually 'lost' back to rich donor nations when medical talents board a plane or sail the Mediterranean Sea and Indian ocean to immigrate. The OECD's current calculation of aid volumes is deceptive and misleading. It does not take into account system 'leakages' like the fruits of development progress i.e. trained medical professionals crossing over to developed countries. A more realistic picture for aid figures would only consider net aid benefits: aid flows minus all benefits accruing to donors from aid recipient countries.

It is possible to correct this imbalance by way of organizing the 'market' for medical professionals from developing nations. The problem with the global recruitment of medical professionals is that it fails the free market test. Because medical care is at the core of human development and as a consequence any socio-economic development experience, it is worth our while examining the forces that affect it and calibrate it properly in order not to jeopardize the hopes of many to meaningfully escape poverty.

Market economists can develop a Health Balance Exchange (HBE) to handle the public international goods that high-skilled health professionals have become. It could work similar to carbon credits that have been developed as part of climate change tackling measures. The Health Balance Exchange will work on the premise that net flows of medical skill are calculated each year and the beneficiaries of the flow are made to pay some compensation to trainer countries. These additional financial flows apart from helping some recognize their albeit unintentional international public service value will help plug some of the holes departing talent have left on the development infrastructure in the form of health facilities, equipment and increased training.

In so doing, the Health Balance Exchange could actually reduce the development aid burden by justifiably converting some and more of it into legitimate flows for marketable services provided in a market that is currently uncontrolled and unregulated, with its large externalities – positive for rich countries and negative for developing ones. The global market for medical professionals is essentially a black market. No equilibrium is in sight. Poor or developing nations cannot compete. All the odds are set against the world's poor as the rich continue the systemic rip off, carting away skilled medical practitioners. The 'trade' is aided by the twin combination of a lure for greener pastures abroad and a disdain for the governance disasters and bad pay at home.

As a result, immigration officers are dealing with a new problem. The pregnant African women sneaking into America, France, the UK or Germany to steal a whiff of advanced medical care for her soon to be delivered baby. Though partly motivated by a desire to give her offspring nationality through *jus soli* for some countries, the underlying rationale remains the same. Being born a national of a rich country grants kids access to superior medical facilities, whenever they will need them in their life. The trend is set to grow, as the middle income group expands in Africa. The market – if we can call it one – does not work. Donor countries of development aid are stealing away the medical human resources that could guarantee good levels of growth and wellbeing for aid recipient countries. A global market regulation is necessary to address the imbalance that ensures rich countries can only attempt to meet their medical staff deficiencies by making African countries and other developing nations even poorer.

It could be argued that creating and promoting such a health market could be counterproductive, resulting in more medical talent being encouraged to sell their expertise to rich countries. This couldn't be more wrong. Firstly, it already exists. The problem is that it is currently a black market. The unwilling or willing cartels are wealthy country governments. This is not an attempt to create an entirely new market. The market is in operation but it is one that escapes all regulation.

What the world should do now is to regulate the market like stock exchanges and some mineral markets are – in order to protect the producers so that they can get a fair price for their labour. If this does not happen, the incentive to produce high quality skilled individuals will continue to fall – with corruption increasing on the other hand as leaders realize that the very little money currently provided them as development aid is insufficient to produce adequate medical facilities. Flights overseas to enjoy first class medical care might be a more enticing option. Immigration to rich Europe will appear more and more like the only fair way to get a life on this earth. You won't blame people for thinking so.

Even the highly corrupt FIFA recognized a very long time ago that grassroots talent producing countries should be compensated each time a player is sold off to a professional league. The system ensures that clubs and schools of football which produce players can use a percentage of the transfer fees to continue operations while the local federation also gets a commission to continue the development of grassroots football. It might not be perfect yet but it is thoroughly sensible. And above all, it is better than the current international theft of medical talent which the world's rich countries are failing to address.

The ideal way to administer remittances from the Health Balance Exchange will be Aid Direct. Its multiple channels will ensure that training schools, health facilities, students, practitioners, patients and central governments get a more or less direct payment from the donor turned buyer. Medical staff who remain in developing countries can then be given a fairer salary that encourages them to stay to serve. Policymakers should contend that for every medical doctor who emigrates to Europe or North America, a silent domino effect would lead to a thousand people of other trades – skilled and unskilled – to follow the immigrant route.

Direction of aid: Faculti

What role could recipient's play in ramping up development efforts? Recipients' strategies for allocating and deploying official development assistance can be significantly improved by a more entrepreneurial and creative approach to addressing development deficiencies. These ought to be used in accordance with local realities. One such programme which could transform the way donors and recipients use aid money to bring lasting change is *Faculti*.

The 'fight against extreme poverty' which rich country governments, NGOs and leaders of developing countries have been priding themselves in is essentially a lie. The world in which poor people live today is fundamentally different from that of half a century ago. There is now no way to escape poverty without first being at least financially literate. This is not necessarily the financial literacy involved in advanced certifications and diplomas or the ability read the markets section of the Economist newsmagazine and make ample sense of it. That level of expertise isn't necessary. That will develop automatically at later stages of the lives of the economically emancipated. This is as simple as understanding how money works, who is involved in money and what personal decisions affect your money and poverty levels.

Financial and Computer Unified Literacy Transformation Initiative – Faculti can help development workers focus resources on what can make a lasting difference. Without appropriate, extensive, adapted and sustained training, the war on poverty is lost. The big mistake has been to fight poverty without first teaching people what poverty is, isn't or helping them understand the simple mechanics of poverty and wealth.

This can be achieved by financial literacy programmes for the young, jobless, adults and poor as a first step to getting out of poverty. Computer education, the other element of Faculti opens doors to the world and prepares people to communicate in our modern times to give them access to the massive opportunities flowing online. These two elements could be combined as one for a preparatory package in the fight against poverty.

The power of compound interest which you may take for granted – you'd be surprised at how many people have no idea what this is all about, talk less of using it to create future wealth. What are banks? What is a credit union? How to calculate profits for your petty business. How to get funding. What is the socio-economic impact of educating your girl child? How to run a small cooperative. How to expand a small business. How to keep costs low.

Is sending an unskilled child overseas, to the streets of America a good investment? How much should I save now to send my children to university in 10 years' time? When is it cheapest to seek medical advice for a health condition? How to draw a budget. How to invest money. How to create wealth. How does money grow? Which crops should I grow? How do I decide what kind of farming to do? The list can run for pages.

These and many more constitute basic knowledge to arm people for their fight against poverty. And this should certainly be a priority area for the channeling of development aid. Every organisation which has been fighting poverty and has not been supporting a financial literacy programme has been wasting its money.

Faculti can be arranged in levels and according to groups. And set up in blocks of 1, 2 or three months per level. It is important to note that the bulk of knowledge and skills in Faculti are not taught in many school systems in developing countries. They are found nowhere, not even in higher education courses. But they ought to be the backbone education for people whose primary challenge is to get out of poverty.

Income generating activities could have up to two times more chance of success when administered to populations that have taken Faculti than to those who have not. If administered to a large number of people, Faculti can be a significant step into getting people out of poverty. It will enable people be responsible for their own socio-economic development.

Adapt Education to Local Circumstances

In developing countries, despite the general low performance on education metrics, imbalance between regions of the same country sometimes show even starker results. In many sub-Saharan countries, the southern, coastal areas tend to perform better than northern Sahel parts on most human development indicators, especially in education and access to social services. Years of neglect, bad governance and politicians' closing their eyes on the tolerance of cultural and traditional practices which have resulted in women being sidelined from education and political participation are to blame.

The growing imbalance between certain regions calls for emergency intervention. The educational gap has been widening in part thanks to a bad copy-and-paste policy that seeks to use the same solutions from the more advanced parts of a country to address educational challenges in regions that should effectively be considered as emergencies. It is all too evident that the two situations cannot have exactly the same solution.

The solution is to properly adapt education to in-country regional circumstances. When development aid for education goes to regions of a country which are in the emergency range, such aid needs to be bolder, innovative and groundbreaking. It should break away from routine. Policy makers should be made to know that the existing policies have failed and the only chance of getting on track is by taking the sensible risk of changing track altogether and adapting education to local needs and circumstances at a large scale.

For example, the education system currently provides for about 7 years of basic education and 6/7 years secondary education in Cameroon and Nigeria. The problem with this model is that northern peoples whose customs take pride in early age productivity for their children do not have the cultural patience to let young people 'waste' 14 years reading books and struggling to pass exams. For women, it's even worse. When parents in that culture do the math, it hits them hard in the face that their daughter will be about 20 when leaving secondary school.

Comparatively, she could have had three to four kids by marrying at 12, plus saving unnecessary expenses like school fees, books and earning the family a fat cow as her dowry. To make matters worse, in their value system, a girl of 20 who is married, has three kids and is helping her husband to grow the clan is surely superior to one who at the same age is battling to pass an exam into higher education. You can disagree with their priorities in life and about when they chose to cross life's big bridges.

Their model has obvious problems for us: child marriage stands out as one of them. That's the way they live, until such time that their own makes the evolutionary shift that hits all social norms, we have to take their current mode of living into consideration. The systematic bashing of everything traditional and not in accordance with 'modern' norms does not help these communities. There is little evidence that any other way of life and value system is superior to theirs.

They have not got the sophistications to reason like others that forging on with school to gain a degree offers better chances of success for women. Success is a culture subjective concept. You think going to school and having a PhD is one of the golden paths of life. Fine. They think starting a family and perpetuating their social norms, avoiding contamination from enticing foreign doctrines is better. For young boys, if their father had given them a bull and a calf as seed money when they were twelve, by 20, they would be running a sizeable herd of profitable animals, not running back to them to ask for money to buy books. Their model has its problems but so do our modern models for progress. The difference must be taken into consideration. That is not asking for too much.

Running campaigns to get parents send all children to school for up to at least high school can help change minds. But this as a solution has failed. The economic arguments and the value system for most of the ethnic groups in the Sahel area is further compounded by high graduate unemployment and low quality jobs barring the less than 5% who stroll into public office and feed themselves fat with embezzled tax payers money … and development aid.

An adapted educational model for such regions should start by recognizing that patience levels for children to get ready for productivity cannot be 14 years of schooling. It is a figure around 10 years and even for this, efforts still have to be made to help parents and the powerful influencers in the community understand the value. When communities understand that they can have their offspring ready for social and economic productivity by age 15/16 rather than 20/21, they will be encouraged to let them pursue education. Girls will be allowed to go to school. Everybody will not be bound to this. There should be two tracks: the traditional 13/14 years and 10 years. How will the 10 year track be implemented?

Firstly, the curriculum should be different. The purpose of the 10 year track is to ensure that pupils are literate, computer literate, financially literate and have sufficient understanding of health, human rights and their environment by the time they complete the third year of secondary education to enable them – for those who desire – to go into skills development and apprenticeships. Their communities will be more supportive when they know their kids are both educated and are learning a trade. These 2 to 3 year apprenticeships and skills development will plug them into their local economy and society faster than the current standard route that leaves a large proportion of youths in their twenties with diplomas and no skills – not even the traditional farming or cattle rearing skills that their parents would have given them, had they not been 'wasting' time in school.

A new curriculum should be developed purposefully with these local realities in mind. The children schooled through this route will also have the advantage that they can always return to education at a later stage in their lives and pursue higher qualifications after years of valuable experience.

Secondly, the new educational track requires a change in the timing of school. Currently, school lasts for nine months in a year of 12. But this is only theoretical. In reality, average actual school time is six and a half months. In order to plug the education gap in these 'emergency' regions, the actual school learning time should move from 6.5 to ten and a half months for the critical three years of secondary education.

Remember that we have deduced the educational patience in those communities to be 7 plus 3 years. The last three years ought to be maximized. The curriculum for the standard 6.5

months (three terms) should be the same as for the rest of the country. This will ensure that there is little disruption in managing two tracks and to leave it open for some to follow the impatient track without losing out on the ability to continue with the standard route patient track.

It is the additional 12 to 15 months freed up within 3 standard academic years that need a special curriculum. This is almost two academic years. Remember this is an emergency and not business as usual. These months of schooling should be focused on life and professional skills training - preparing the students to take skills based qualifications – something like NVQ (National Vocational Qualification) levels 1 and 2. This will include our suite of world citizenship courses: computer and financial literacy, human rights and development, health and environment. And because parents will see their children studying academically and also learning some of the life skills like cattle rearing, arts and craft, agriculture, tailoring, shop management, etc which they cherish so much, will be encouraged to support their education.

They will be proud of their kids who at 16 will be better rounded individuals with academic, social and economic skills. If this is properly implemented as part of the aid pillars, the threshold age of marriage for girls will with easy cultural acceptability shift from 11/12 to 16/17. Early and forced marriage could as such be significantly reduced. Of course all this needs to be funded to ensure universal coverage in the regions concerned. But the starting point is recognizing that one size doesn't fit all in education and that patience levels exist, which determine how long societies are willing to keep children especially girls in school. Education should match patience levels and not vice versa.

To conclude, there should be a strong dimension to prepare aid receiving communities to adapt to the end of aid by teaching creativity, innovation and entrepreneurship.

Global Aid, not Development Aid

Development aid is a smoke screen. It should be rightly called global aid. The boomerang effects of development aid that have resulted in overwhelming benefits to donor countries as opposed to the supposed beneficiaries has unquestionably morphed development aid into what it really is: global aid. A good proportion of what development aid is attempting to address are problems created, enhanced, or that could be propagated by the dynamics of globalization.

More and more, countries are using development aid to promote their security, safety and prosperity interests. Should we appropriately term this 'global aid' rather than 'development aid'?

The aid industry has created and sustained hundreds of thousands of white collar jobs in donor countries, benefiting donor country citizens. The consultancies that carry out development work are all based in … you guess where. Aid payments returning to or simply never leaving the rich donor country far exceeds that which trickles down to the beneficiary in Africa and still exceeds the value of any services provided for the money.

Development Evangelism led by local town councils

Councils should not lock themselves up in their councils. Africa needs more development evangelists than churches need 'prophets'. Mayors, councilors, local civil society need to come out to challenge the way development aid is currently being misused. They can play a strong role in advocating for what rightly should be the place of local councils in the development process.

For too long, centralization and out of touch politicians and policy makers have taken the development process hostage in severely corrupt and bureaucracy ridden national capitals. Councils do have their own problems. Despite their nepotism, weak governance and lack of capacity, they still manage to deliver projects faster, cheaper and with greater local engagement than central governments. The town council has to be the heartbeat of the development process.

A new role for multilateral donors

The question every organization employing itself in the development of Africa should be asking itself everyday is: are we serving Africa's people? It is one question without a definite answer. Even the best responses will vary in space and time. The UN and the World Bank can find a more potent role in actually enabling the development by process by becoming matchmakers, proponents and watchdogs for equality in the development process around the world.

The fact that development efforts have largely failed is evidence of the shortcomings of organisations like the IMF, World Bank and several others – among them some UN bodies – in helping countries stand up and walk their progress with confidence and benefits for their people. No meaningful positive change will take place in Africa if these bodies which often call the shots or have the influence to, do not review their engagement manual with the continent, its institutions and its people.

The people in developing countries should be at the core of any development, cooperation or advisory work carried out by global institutions. Currently, it appears greater effort is made by international organisations to appear politically correct in the face of the host government or foster some economic and monetary policy cooked in the drawers of rich, developed shareholders than the interest of local people who bear the brunt of underdevelopment.

The overriding result is a requiem mass for democracy and a further lease for corruption. Instead of governments to work to meet the desires and expectations of their electorate, they focus the muscle of their technocrats in meeting naught but the demands of these big donor agencies. The problem is that despite maybe the good intentions of donors and lenders, the latter pair may not understand the unintended harm they are causing. It is common sight in Africa to come across a street banner congratulating the recipient country's president for a road funded by development agencies or hospitals built by Japan, Korea or China. Unscrutinised aid and a blind following of the edicts of donors and lenders is a sure affront to democracy.

In another example, the IMF comes to an African country, where about half the people live on lower than two dollars a day and mounts pressure on government to end fuel subsidies. Its 'experts' arrogantly proclaim that this is sound economic advice. Of course there are benefits to reducing and even ending subsidies. Fuel subsidies tend to benefit the rich rather than the poor in less developed countries. That is one of the numerous recommendations the IMF makes on host governments. Although there have not been equally strong calls for Europe, for example, to end subsidies to farmers.

Then the same organization goes to Washington DC for a similar mission: advice the US government on economic growth. The IMF warns President Barack Obama's administration to raise the minimum wage. Africans would not believe their ears. Hundreds of millions of African citizens have been fighting with governments for years, trying to persuade them increase the minimum wage. For a track record of clientelist, subjective and biased advisory some rich donor agencies are regarded by many informed observers as organisations which are not interested in the actual development of developing countries. Their interests lie in 'stabilising' the global economy, irrespective of whom this 'stabilisation' actually benefits.

When prescribing pills to ailing African 'economies', there a number of things donors and lenders of both cash, expertise and ideas should keep in the front of their thinking. African countries are more than economies – in fact every country is more than an economy of numbers. African countries are societies. Secondly, these organisations must thread with caution when dealing with Africa. High handed assurance and patriarchal approaches must be banished. Partners should engage with the clear realization that they could be at least half wrong.

The complexity of each African country's fabric is not a subject that has expert masters and this is partly because African people are suffering a double dictatorship. They suffer the dictatorship of their 'elected' governments – usually westernized African elites. Then have also got the diktats of the big multilateral organisations which have arrogated to themselves expert status on African development matters. Because none of these powerful dictatorial forces are really listening to the African woman, child and man, there are hardly any claimable experts on Africa in the midst of both pairs of dictatorial regiments. Each dictator appears driven only by their own survival instinct.

If international development agencies want to be counted among the pivotal brokers of development, they should consider a switch in their central objectives when it comes to their dealings with Africa. What the countries in the continent need now is sincere development evangelists and practitioners, the organizations who can reach out to impact the lives of the people who suffer more from the policy decisions that have been made over the last half century.

Development agencies should be preoccupied with helping African governments to rapidly reach high levels of monetary governance similar to those of developed countries but without committing the mistakes that have periodically threatened to kill the global economy. How paradoxical that African countries with proven gold reserves in their soil are told that they do not have reserves to keep their currency stable. Or maybe these reserves and deposits are not proven after all.

International development banks should be saying to a number of African countries, 'you need to build your own replica of the Massachusetts Institute of Technology and by the way we can help you gather partners to support your delivery of your MIT'. The Massachusetts Institute of Technology has been such a pivotal element in America's drive to technical superiority in the world that several other leaders in 'advanced' countries envied and sought to copy it. It is amazing that for all the billions of dollars and high level expertise the rich are throwing out to developing countries, building the robust technical institutions which can sustainably ensure wealth creation in these countries is not top of the agenda.

They should go to local councils and say, where is that housing project of yours? Is there something we can do together about your city transport network? Can we broker a really quick and effective knowledge transfer deal between you and Milton Keynes or London? Does Bristol in the UK want to partner with Buea in Cameroon, Dire Dawa in Ethiopia and Nsukka in Nigeria and Nyeri in Kenya for frank development skills exchange and resources sharing? Can the UNDP, UNESCO and World Bank come into the middle of all this and say 'we'll help you strike a deal and provide the resources for you to learn, share and grow for the benefit of your communities?

Development coaching spiced with finding potent partners for development mentoring could become the core activity of international development agencies. This could make these bodies more responsive to the aspirations of the peoples in these struggling democracies. And critically, it should keep them slim to the core, thus releasing a flood of billions into the development space.

These approaches, despite their obvious benefits in adding value may still prove not to meet the optimum effort for attaining global development. However, they appear amenable and would still meet the secret requirement of several dark lobbyists in the undercurrent of development aid policy making in that it ensures long term reciprocity.

But is there an ideal aid model which can cut the debate?

Chapter VI The Churchill – Fleming Aid Model

If the evil that men do lives after them, surely the good they do lives with them.

Did the lives of two famous Britons intersect? An incident in Scotland several decades ago may just have offered a path to salvage development aid, plug its prejudices and turn its heart to deliver effective sustainable development. Here is a version of the story as popularly believed.

The Power of a Good Deed

It must have been one of those soggy cold times when the highlands all seem taken over by hideous hidden bayous either sent by gods for minor life to thrive or by fiends for anything that breathes to fall prey to.

Fleming had set off to farm early in one of the Scottish woods where poor farmers lived off the fruits of a daily hustle between their hands and the good fertile earth. He would work hard and mumble a tune to himself, enjoying every bit of the struggle. He would sometimes use the wind's gentle whirls to rhyme a verse that was knocking in his head. Every now and then, he would pause, drop his tools, step a few yards back and nod with smug approval at the distance he had beaten, tilling, clearing and planting.

One day, as he paused for his muscles to refresh, he thought he heard a noise from the woods. It wasn't a squirrel. It wasn't a stray dog. He heard it again. It was a boy's scream. A scream for help. A scream that pierced his ears, heart and ruffled his spine.

The baffled man fumbled around the bush to trace the source. His battered boots led him to an open clearing in the bush which his experienced head instantly marked as dangerous. Trap marsh liked open clearings, spots tempting enough to mislead the untrained forest wanderer into thinking this is spot for a green picnic.

A boy was stuck in the bog. He was mired waist down in wet dirt unpleasant to look at. His eyes bore the look of terror at an impending death. He'd been drained dry of energy after several failed attempts to wiggle his way out of the quagmire. His hands were now just hanging hopelessly in the air like pennants of a vanquished army pondering the terms of its surrender. As old Fleming's cap popped at the marsh, the boy launched one more vocal that set a few small animals scampering for cover.

Farmer Fleming used a farming tug rope and a stick to pull the lad out and so saved him from a slow and painful departure from the land of the living.

By the time Fleming returned the boy to the latter's family estate and regain his own small dwelling, news had spread around the boroughs of one farmer's heroism. There was disappointment for passersby as he trod back home, unwilling to discuss the adventure with anyone. He turned down any pint offer at the pub that evening. He knew all they wanted was a fine tale of his struggle to wrestle a boy from the hands of the devil, a beast or three witches depending on the gossip strand that thrived in your street.

The following day, before he could finish lacing his boots for the long trip to his farm, a fancy carriage pulled up to the Scotman's modest dwelling. An elaborately dressed nobleman came out and scanned the surroundings as if he had come for a buyer's inspection. "I am the father of the lad you saved," the big man introduced himself to Farmer Fleming. "You saved my son's life. I can't be indifferent. I want to pay you back."

"I can't accept payment for what I did. Anyone would have saved him," the farmer swept away the offer, almost breaking into a smile.

"You are a hero. You deserve recognition and gratitude. I can give you –" the nobleman was charging again before Fleming interrupted, lifting his hand.

"Your son, sir, is the hero. He fought to stay alive. He wanted to live and he hoped someone would find him. I won't take anything from you."

The visitor was just about defeated. He stood there wondering what to do, with a still open carriage waiting to pour his largesse. That is the moment when the farmer's son came through the door of the family hut.

"Is that your boy?" The visitor asked.

Fleming nodded and turned around to stare at his son cheerfully. He was about to tell a small funny story about his

boy to the visitor but the man in several well tailored dressing bits spoke before him.
"I'll make you a deal. This has been a hard but quick lesson. I do understand you are a man of principles, the sort of values my club members seek and cherish. Let me provide your son with the level of education my own son will enjoy. If the lad has got an element of his brave father in him, he'll surely grow to a man who will make the land proud."

Farmer Fleming accepted the arrangement. He saw it as a chance for his boy to experience another part of the borough, build friendships and learn the art of living with people.

Farmer Fleming's son went on to attend some very good schools and later graduated from St. Mary's Hospital Medical School in London. He then went on to grow in fame and be known around the world as Sir Alexander Fleming, the discoverer of penicillin.

Years later, the son of the nobleman who had been saved from the bog was suffering from a pneumonia attack. The penicillin discovered by his first rescuer's son saved his life this time. The noblemen was Lord Randolph Churchill. His son was Sir Winston Churchill.

How can development aid be modeled on Churchill-Fleming?

In several respects, this is a touching story. It's so beautiful you'll wish it happened ever so often in people's lives. But let's be clear that this story is almost certainly fiction, stuff of legend, as many have pointed out already. The Churchill Foundation refutes it. The Churchill Foundation has set out clearly how unlikely it is for the events to have actually happened. But whether it is fiction or reality is of little importance. The strong point here is that this simple story of positive karma, a circle of goodness and the surety of interdependence between the rich powerful and the weak poor provides policy makers with what could arguably be called the perfect or near perfect development model on a miniature scale.

In more ways than one, the *Chufle*[3] encounter resembles our simplified world with its development challenges.

When Churchill tried to force a gift onto Senior Fleming, the goodhearted man refused to take it. He didn't want to be repaid for his good work. He had acted on principle in saving a man's life. He might have been struggling in cash terms. But he was healthy in spirit and at heart and certainly wealthy in life's principles and self esteem. Africans should with dignity and friendship politely reject senseless aid.

Aid that builds the numbers, aid that will be held up in annual reports and conferences around the globe as evidence of benevolence to suffering peoples, aid that will be used to create a moral debt that leads to other things, aid which as we know returns to the donor, aid which is a badly calculated bribe to stay off Europe's and America's shores, aid that seals bruises and leave ulcers bare. Recipient countries should wear Senior Fleming's battered cloak and selfless spirit. Confine aid that serves no purpose other than sustaining the international aid industry and political psyche soothing to the dustbin. This is a pivotal recipient role.

Aid has to be finite or bidirectional. Africa should with dignity reject aid that will be perpetual. Perpetual superficially unidirectional aid is bondage to both benefactor and beneficiary. Aid that ensures the charity business in the UK

[3] Chufle = Churchill-Fleming

and Germany continue to scramble for top spot with manufacturing and tourism in the economy should be ditched.

Farmer Fleming could have accepted payment for his life-saving action. That would have been the first tranche of a development programme that might have been running up till this day. It would have resulted in some of Churchill's offspring specializing in handing over annual packages of essential supplies to the Flemings. The Fleming offspring would have grown so accustomed to these supplies that they would have had several of their kinsmen with hands trained for nothing else save reception of 'kindness'. These hands won't even be trained for the farm work that had led their ancestor to the fields and to eventually find a boy to save.

Eventually, there would be years when the benefactor's estate won't produce enough for the Churchills to justify any significant generosity. The Flemings would suffer in those years. Several other things could go wrong. Entire vocations could be lost. Some Flemings might think it is now noble to abandon their decaying estate to mow the lawn at the Churchills' instead.

Penicillin would eventually have been discovered anyways. But it may have taken four more generations of Churchill's to produce a medical researcher with the chance to land on the bactericide phenomenon or who knows; its discoverer might have instead arisen from Berlin, Paris or elsewhere.

Churchill attempted to take the chance to put himself and potentially his offspring in bondage of perpetual support. Fleming rescued him from that also. As he finally embraced the option of life time, finite and optimum quality aid, he inadvertently put himself and his offspring at a point on the arc of aid's circular economy that permitted himself and the Flemings to receive some direct dividends for themselves, for mankind and with the added satisfaction that a seed planted several years back like a trivial act has grown into a tree of life within a generation.

The next lesson we learn from the Churchill – Fleming model is one you expect every parent to have taught their children: dignity in the conditions of your life, however modest they may be. Don't be envious of material trappings. This might sound like your granny's voice. Strive to have more of what you really need with your own means. Africans should quickly come to the realization that not everything that rich countries have, lead to happiness. This is not the apology of poverty. Wealth is great and is surely one of humanity's great missions. Poor countries should seek wealth with haste, passion but also with wisdom and heart. The purpose for owning wealth should be the focus. Wealth's mission and its method of attainment should all be noble. And to understand that there is other wealth which 'experts' fail to theorize on is superior economic understanding.

Churchill was embarrassed when his offer of a thank you gift was turned down. He probably didn't meet such dignified human spirits so easily. And so he took interest. He changed the offer. 'I will educate your son to the same standard as mine'. When Africa will reject cosmetic aid, donor countries will think about real aid. Notice how Churchill used no prejudice. He didn't bother that taking up responsibility for Fleming's son will lead the poor farmer to start a children hatch farm with his wife or another woman in the hope that their son's benefactor will extend more help. Churchill didn't create prejudice. He didn't pose conditions – well the only obligations he placed were upon his own self. He gave himself the obligation to treat the farmer's son equally as he treated his own offspring.

Churchill didn't turn up at the next town meeting to announce his righteousness. He simply kept to his task. Churchill and

Fleming have exemplified sustainable aid in a way you might not find in textbook theories. Their exchange was dignified, it was selfless but finally procured benefits for both men and for the wider society. That's what development aid or rather global aid should look like.

The Churchill – Fleming Aid Model teaches another important lesson. Aid should not be a figure but a purpose. Aid should not be a number but a mission. Aid is always tied to financial cycles. Another big mistake. Fleming's son obtained from Churchill as much aid as he needed to become a final product – a medical innovator. He didn't get a fixed proportion of the Churchill's income. It was not conditional on a famine to hit the Flemings. It wasn't tied to revenue or the harvest season. It was round the clock. We should imagine that there were years when fortunes slipped slightly and the whole household had to survive on a few pounds less. Yes, but that would have affected even Churchill's own biological children.

How Churchill set the quality standard for the aid that he gave to Fleming is really interesting. He may have had over a hundred options. He could have said 'I'll pay your fees at school every year'. That, I think would be good enough. If this alone was offered to every African girl or boy who wanted to go to school, we wouldn't be squabbling about development aid at the UN this much in twenty five years from now. Even this highly acceptable version of aid is not available to those who need it.

The man could also go 'Okay, Mister Fleming, I understand you are a dignified and principled man. But could you come see me in my office anytime you have a problem? You know, I'll be willing to support you. If anything bothers you, just come see me and we can talk about it together'. I guess he would wonder if the man will ever come, even if his son was on a dying bed. Or maybe he sensed Fleming had placed the bar of dignity so high he felt aroused to match it with something equally gold in standard.

Churchill could have taken up medical bills for Fleming, say even for a decade, two or a lifetime. In our politically frightened world today, even such a model would be utopic, especially as several 'wealthy' country governments are failing their own citizens in providing reasonable medical care or even basic health education. But this alone would have put the Churchill aid on a pedestal and there won't be a handful today to topple that. There isn't yet a race of politicians in the developed world who would see things this way, at least publicly. There are honest people in western political capitals who unfortunately have to toe party lines and put up with a political discipline that is not compatible with their deepest beliefs and values concerning aid. That is part of the tragedy of aid as a political orphan, a child only the insignificant minority might be willing to accommodate.

There was another option. Churchill could ensure that the Fleming boy is never hungry. Wouldn't it be great to live your life, managing with school knowing that you'll never hungry and thirst? In many parts of Africa, when kids are in school, their biggest source of distraction is the constant worry from midday whether or not they will meet a half decent meal when they return home at the end of the day. In secondary schools, the bigger students have reduced their school attendance to match their attention levels to just the first three hours of the school day. They've got a long way to trek back home and not even be sure if a meal will be available. Guaranteed meals for little Fleming, even if his father went bankrupt would have been a shining light in their lives.

Churchill ignored all these options. In a moment of genius, audacity and perhaps a bit of madness, he aspired for something more human or even a little bit beyond, something that would embarrass most of today's leaders. He opted for lifetime aid. The old man picked a really strange quality standard. 'I will give your son the same care and education which mine will have'. Fictional Churchill deserves a standing ovation at this point.

The *Chufle* model could be a way by which the world solves its development challenges, sustainably and indefinitely. The model ensures a reciprocal and circular flow of goodness (development benefits) and recognizes that the global development marketplace is a single ecosystem. The countries, zones, sub-regions, and areas whether mountain high in wealth or full of social chaos are all living elements of an ecosystem where shocks start from one end and relapse in the other.

Conclusion

Churchill didn't offer 0.01, 0.7% or 2% of his domestic income. He offered aid that had no number. No target spend. No prejudice. No name. We can call it lifetime aid. Aid of infinite quality, determined only by the ability, sincerity of purpose and audacity of the benefactor on the one hand and the availability and hard work of the recipient on the other hand to make good on the opportunity afforded both for the sustainable development of mankind.

Part of the problem with today's development aid is multiple standards. The idea that there is one quality of healthcare and education that is acceptable for Africans and another separate, higher and advanced version that Europeans, Japanese and Americans aspire to is a regrettable error in development planning and objective setting. Churchill and Fleming have shown albeit on a laboratory scale that the best aid that works is similar standards for both donor and recipient, not half measures. Has the world produced the politicians and technocrats who can square up to the day's challenge, change their attitudes and mindset on development or global aid?

Double and multiple standards aid will ensure the continuous growth of the aid industry into perpetuity without a decline in sight. This will destroy any hopes of sustainability in the aid mechanism. If aid targets are not set to the point where they attain a marginal utility that equals zero, just at the point before which they reach diminishing returns, development aid will not be sustainable in the long run. While it is perfectly sensible to have interim objectives in the aid mechanism, any final objective premised on the hope that disparate qualities of development are acceptable depending on where you are on the planet are bound to fail. We should contend and be frightened that in another 15 years, we'll still be here with the failed Sustainable Development Goals staring in the face of mankind, its politicians, its technocrats and bureaucrats. And perhaps when the history of aid is rewritten in the century after ours, we might not exactly be recognized as homo sapiens.

References

Tweedy, N (2013), Bill Gates interview: I have no use for money. This is God's work, retrieved from The Telegraph website www.telegraph.co.uk, 18 Jan 2013

By December 2015, the Bill and Melinda Gates Foundation had spent 34.5 billion USD on global development*

Bill and Melinda Gates Foundation, Foundation factsheet, retrieved from the Gates Foundation website www.gatesfoundation.org, 2 Dec 2015

The Office of Tony Blair, What we do, retrieved from The Office of Tony Blair website www.tonyblairoffice.org, 02 December 2015

Moyo, D. (2010) Dead Aid, Penguin Books

Page 8 Dambisa Moyo 8 Jan 2011, The Telegraph, www.telegraph.co.uk

Macgroarty, P. and Flynn, A. (2013, April), UK to End South Africa Aid in 2015, retrieved from Wall Street Journal website www.wsj.com on 2 December 2015

Deaton, A. (2013, September) The Great Escape: Health, Wealth and the Origins of Inequality, Princeton, New Jersey, Princeton University Press

Der Spiegel
Independent Commission for Aid, (May 2012) DFID's Education Programmes in Three East African Countries, Report 10

Ministry of Information, Cultural Affairs and Tourism, Government of Liberia (2015), retrieved from website http://www.micatliberia.com/

Easterly, W., Pfutze, T. (Spring 2008) Where Does the Money Go? Best and Worst Practices in Foreign Aid Journal of Economic Perspectives, Vol. 22, No. 2, retrieved from New York University website www.nyu.edu

The Annual Report on Philantropy (2015), Giving Statistics, retrieved from the website of Charity Navigator www.charitynavigator.org on 2 December 2015

Kharas, H., (2007, November) "Trends and Issues in Development Aid", Working paper, Washington DC, Wolfensohn Center for Development at the Brookings Institution

Phillips, A. D. (2013) Development Without Aid – The Decline of Development Aid and the Rise of the Diaspora, London, Anthem Press

Provost, Claire; The Guardian, 7 Sep 2011, theguardian.com

OECD History of 0.7% target,

Booth, Lorna; The 0.7% aid target, 24 July 2014, SN/EP/3714, House of Commons Library

Christian Concerns in Economic and Social Development, August 21-29, 1958, Appendix XIV, p. 125. – cited in OECD, Development Co-operation, 1999 Report)

Development aid by countries has hardly exceeded 0.4%
Norbert Neusser on Euractiv.com
Collier, Paul, The Bottom Billion, Oxford University Press, 2007

Der Spiegel
Birell, 2004 (UK aid to education in Ethiopia, Rwanda and Tanzania fails to improve anything …)

Kraise, K. (2010) True Size of Africa, public domain

Poverty's long farewell, (2015, Feb 28) The Economist, retrieved from www.economist.com

The world's next great leap forward – Towards the end of poverty, (2013, Jun 1) The Economist, retrieved from www.economist.com

Ntale, C. L., (2013, October) "Where does aid money really go – and what is it spent on?", Cable News Network website www.cnn.com, retrieved on 03 Dec 2015

Craig, D. (2014, November) 'The Great British rake … what actually happens to the billions you donate to charity: Fat cat pay, appalling waste and hidden agendas', retrieved from the Daily Mail website www.dailymail.co.uk 3 December 2015

Keen, R. Charities and the voluntary sector, Briefing Paper Number SN05428 (2015, July) London, United Kingdom, House of Commons Library (2015)

Moyo, D. (2009, March) Why Foreign Aid Is Hurting Africa, retrieved from The Wall Street Journal website www.wsj.com on 3 Dec 2015

World Urbanization Prospects – 2014 Revision, (2014), United Nations

Chandy, L., Ledlie, N. & Penciakova, V. (2013, April) "The Final Countdown: Prospects for Ending Extreme Poverty by 2030", Washington: DC, The Brookings Institution

United States Environmental Protection Agency. (2007, May 4). Climate Change. Retrieved From the Environmental Protection Agency website: http://www.epa.gov/climatechange
In-text reference: (United States Environmental, 2007)

www.ingramcontent.com/pod-product-compliance
Lightning Source LLC
Chambersburg PA
CBHW070255190526
45169CB00001B/420

* 9 7 8 1 5 3 0 1 9 6 9 8 2 *